"If slaughterhouses had glass walls, everyone would be vegetarian. We feel better about ourselves and better about the animals knowing that we are not contributing to their pain."
— Linda McCartney

"I brainwashed youngsters into doing wrong. I want to say sorry to children everywhere for selling out to concerns who make millions by murdering animals."
— Geoffrey Giuliano, the main Ronald McDonald actor in the 1980s, in his public apology, after quitting his job.

"Nothing will benefit human health and increase the chances for survival of life on Earth as much as the evolution to a vegetarian diet."
— Albert Einstein

"The meat industry spends hundreds of millions of dollars lying to the public about their product. But no amount of false propaganda can sanitize meat. The facts are absolutely clear: Eating meat is bad for human health, catastrophic for the environment, and a living nightmare for animals."
— Chrissie Hynde, singer/songwriter of the Pretenders

"If you are as you have described yourself the king of the animals – it would be better for you to call yourself king of the beasts since you are the greatest of them all! – because you help them only so that they may presently be able to give you their young in order to gratify your palate, for the sake of which you have tried to make yourself a tomb for all the animals. Even more I might say if to speak the entire truth were permitted me.... Now does not nature produce enough simple vegetarian food for you to satisfy yourself?"
— Leonardo da Vinci

Books by His Divine Grace
A. C. Bhaktivedanta Swami Prabhupāda

Bhagavad-gītā As It Is
Śrīmad-Bhāgavatam (completed by disciples)
Śrī Caitanya-caritāmṛta
Kṛṣṇa, the Supreme Personality of Godhead
Teachings of Lord Caitanya
The Nectar of Devotion
The Nectar of Instruction
Śrī Īśopaniṣad
Light of the Bhāgavata
Easy Journey to Other Planets
Teachings of Lord Kapila, the Son of Devahūti
Teachings of Queen Kuntī
Message of Godhead
The Science of Self-Realization
The Perfection of Yoga
Beyond Birth and Death
On the Way to Kṛṣṇa
Rāja-vidyā: The King of Knowledge
Elevation to Kṛṣṇa Consciousness
Kṛṣṇa consciousness: The Matchless Gift
Kṛṣṇa consciousness: The Topmost Yoga System
Perfect Questions, Perfect Answers
Life Comes from Life
The Nārada-bhakti-sūtra (completed by disciples)
The Mukunda-mālā-stotra (completed by disciples)
Geetār-gān (Bengali)
Vairāgya-vidyā (Bengali)
Buddhi-yoga (Bengali)
Bhakti-ratna-boli (Bengali)
Back to Godhead magazine (founder)

Books compiled from the teachings of His Divine Grace
A. C. Bhaktivedanta Swami Prabhupāda after his lifetime

Search for Liberation
A Second Chance
The Journey of Self-Discovery
Civilization and Transcendence
The Laws of Nature
Renunciation Through Wisdom
The Quest for Enlightenment
Dharma, the Way of Transcendence
Beyond Illusion and Doubt
Bhakti, the Art of Eternal Love
Spiritual Yoga
The Hare Kṛṣṇa Challenge

The Higher Taste

A Guide to Gourmet Vegetarian Cooking and a Karma-Free Diet

Based on the teachings of
His Divine Grace
A. C. Bhaktivedanta Swami
Prabhupāda
Founder-Ācārya of the International Society
for Krishna Consciousness

THE BHAKTIVEDANTA BOOK TRUST

Readers interested in the subject matter of this book
are invited to correspond with the publisher at one
of the following addresses:

The Bhaktivedanta Book Trust
P.O. Box 341445, Los Angeles, CA 90034, USA
Phone: +1 800 927 4152 • Fax: +1 310 837 1056
E-mail: bbt.usa@krishna.com

ISKCON Reader Services
P.O. Box 730, Watford, WD25 8ZE, United Kingdom
E-mail: readerservices@pamho.net
Website: www.iskcon.org.uk

The Bhaktivedanta Book Trust
P.O. Box 380, Riverstone, NSW 2765, Australia
Phone: +61 2 96276306 • Fax: +61 2 96276052
E-mail: bbt.wp@krishna.com

www.krishna.com

Cover design: Raghu Consbruck
Recipes: Kūrma Dāsa
Editorial supervision: Kaiśorī Dāsī
Color illustration: Rāmadāsa Abhirāma Dāsa and Dhṛti Dāsī

Copyright © 1983, 2006
The Bhaktivedanta Book Trust International, Inc.

Recipes on pages 67–69, 18–88, 91–96, 100, 101, 103–106, 120,132
133, 137, 140, 147, 150, 151 copyright © 1990 Bhaktivedanta Books Inc.

Other recipes copyright © 1990–2000 Philip Gordon

Food photography copyright © 1990–2000 Bhaktivedanta Books Inc.

ISBN 978-1-84599-047-3

Previous printings: 720,000
Current printing, 2021: 100,000

Printed in China

We dedicate this book to our beloved
spiritual master and guide, His Divine Grace
A. C. Bhaktivedanta Swami Prabhupāda,
who brought the transcendental teachings
of Lord Kṛṣṇa to the Western world.

"Thousands of people who say they 'love' animals sit down once or twice a day to enjoy the flesh of creatures who have been utterly deprived of everything that could make their lives worth living and who endured the awful suffering and the terror of the abattoirs."

— Dr. Jane Goodall, PhD,
conservationist and primatologist

Contents

Introduction

"Influenced by factors ranging from health and economics to ethics and religion, millions of people around the world are turning to a vegetarian diet. In America alone, one in ten persons considers him or herself a vegetarian. The same is true in the United Kingdom. Actually, five thousand people a week in Britain are becoming vegetarians. For more than twenty years, *The Higher Taste* has been one of the most widely distributed introductions to vegetarianism. The editors are pleased to provide you here with an improved edition with all-new recipes, including elegant vegan choices and a number of reduced-fat or low-fat recipes.

The Higher Taste looks at some of the reasons why people stop eating meat. Also offered here are more than fifty gourmet vegetarian recipes guaranteed to carry you beyond the pleasures of ordinary food into a new realm of epicurean delight. If you ever thought being vegetarian meant eating steamed vegetables and cold salads, you're in for a surprise. In *The Higher Taste* you'll learn to prepare complete, nourishing, taste-tempting, and healthful meals based on world cuisine. Visit the cooking of Latin America, Europe, Asia, and the Middle East in these pages. These tested recipes have been chosen for their ease of preparation and their cosmopolitan flair.

About the Title

For those looking to improve the quality of their lives, how a meal is prepared is just as important as the ingredients that go into it. When performed in proper consciousness, cooking can be as satisfying and conducive to good health as any other form of meditation. In India's ancient wisdom text, the *Bhagavad-gītā*, Lord Kṛṣṇa explains, "If one offers Me with love and devotion a leaf, a flower, a fruit or water, I will accept it."

Followers of the *Bhagavad-gītā* know that preparing and then offering pure, natural vegetarian food to the Supreme creates a feeling of sublime pleasure in the heart. Cooking becomes yoga. That's what we mean by a "higher taste."

The Logic of Vegetarianism

The opening chapters of *The Higher Taste* explain the philosophy behind spiritual and ethical vegetarianism.

Chapter One reveals how modern medical research links meat-eating with killer diseases such as cancer and heart disease. Chapter Two exposes the myth of a worldwide food scarcity and explains the economic advantages of a vegetarian diet. In Chapter Three, the ethical foundations of vegetarianism are set forth, focusing on the writings of distinguished philosophers, authors, and religious leaders. The principle of nonviolence as found in the teachings of Judaism, Christianity, Buddhism, and Hinduism is also examined. An analysis of how the laws of karma and reincarnation are related to vegetarianism forms the basis of Chapter Four. Chapter Five explains the rationale behind and the procedures for offering vegetarian food to the Supreme Lord as part of the *bhakti-yoga* system. Chapter Six offers excerpts from the writings of His Divine Grace A. C. Bhaktivedanta Swami Prabhupāda, India's greatest authority on Vedic devotional culture, and provides a concise, readable summary of the philosophy underlying the spiritual vegetarian diet outlined in *The Higher Taste*.

Apart from being a prolific author, Śrīla Prabhupāda, as he is known, also founded the International Society for Krishna Consciousness in 1966. See page 158 of this book for an overview of the Kṛṣṇa consciousness movement's varied food- related activities – vegetarian restaurants, self-sufficient farm communities, public festivals with free feasts, and more."

1

Health and a Meatless Diet

"I don't understand why asking people to eat a well-balanced vegetarian diet is considered drastic, while it is medically conservative to cut people open."

— Dr. Dean Ornish, MD, founder, president, and director of The Preventative Medicine Research Institute, Sausalito, CA, and author of *Dr. Dean Ornish's Program for Reversing Heart Disease*

With increasing evidence of diet's critical role in finding or maintaining good health, more and more people are investigating vegetarianism. When comparing the benefits of a vegetarian diet to a meat-based diet, two areas should be considered – the anatomical structure of the human body, and the physical effects of meat consumption. Since eating begins with the hands and mouth, the anatomy of these bodily parts can tell us something. Human teeth, like those of all herbivores, are designed for grinding and chewing. Humans lack the sharp canine teeth designed for tearing flesh that are characteristic of all carnivores. Meat-eating animals generally swallow their food without chewing it, so they require neither molars nor sideways-moving jaws. And the human hand, with its opposable thumb and lack of sharp claws, is better suited to harvesting fruits and vegetables than to killing prey.

Digesting Meat

Once it has been swallowed, meat requires digestive juices high in hydrochloric acid to break it down. The stomachs of humans and other herbivores produce less than one-twentieth of the acid produced by carnivores.

The intestinal tracts of meat-eaters and vegetarians also differ. Meat is dead flesh, and flesh begins to putrefy almost instantly upon death. When flesh is consumed, this putrefaction poisons the body. That's why carnivores have to eliminate their meals quickly – why they have digestive tracts only three times the length of their bodies. Since humans, like non–flesh-

Physiological Comparisons

Meat-eater	Herbivore	Human
Has claws	No claws	No claws
No skin pores, perspires through tongue	Perspires through skin pores	Perspires through skin pores
Sharp front teeth for tearing, no flat molar teeth for grinding	No sharp front teeth; has flat rear molars	No sharp front teeth; has flat rear molars
Intestinal tract 3 times body length so rapidly decaying meat can pass out quickly	Intestinal tract 10–12 times body length	Intestinal tract 12 times body length
Strong hydrochloric acid in stomach to digest meat	Stomach acid 20 times weaker than meat-eater's	Stomach acid 20 times weaker than meat-eater's

eating animals, have digestive tracts twelve times the length of their bodies, the rapidly decaying flesh in a meat-based meal is retained for much longer, producing a number of toxic effects.

One organ adversely affected by these toxins is the kidney. This vital organ, which extracts wastes from the blood, is strained by the overload of poisons meat consumption introduces. The kidneys of even moderate meat-eaters must work three times harder than the kidneys of vegetarians. Young people's kidneys may be able to cope with this added stress, but as one grows older, the risk of kidney disease and finally kidney failure increases.

The pancreas is also adversely affected by the toxins. True carnivores eat their meat raw; humans prefer the taste of cooked meat. Cooking destroys the natural enzymes present in the meat that aid a carnivore's digestion. The pancreas must therefore produce more digestive enzymes, gradually stressing the organ, weakening it, and inviting disease.

Heart Disease

The inability of the human body to deal with excessive animal fats in the diet is another indication of the unnaturalness of meat-eating. Carnivorous animals can metabolize almost unlimited amounts of cholesterol and fat without adverse effects. In experiments with dogs, up to half a pound of butterfat was added to their daily diet over a period of two years, producing absolutely no change in their serum cholesterol level.

On the other hand, herbivorous species have a very limited ability to deal with any cholesterol or saturated fat beyond what the body actually requires. When over a period of many years an excess is consumed, fatty deposits (plaque) accumulate on the inner walls of the arteries, producing a condition known as atherosclerosis, or hardening of the arteries. Because the plaque deposits constrict the flow of blood to the heart, the potential for heart attacks, strokes, and blood clots is tremendously increased.

Marion Nestle, Chair of the Nutrition Department at New York University, states, "Meat contributes an extraordinarily significant percentage of the saturated fat in the American diet." As early as 1961, the *Journal of the American Medical Association* stated that 97 percent of heart disease cases, the cause of more than one half of the deaths in the United States, could be prevented by a vegetarian diet. These findings are supported by an American Heart Association report that high-saturated-fat diets cause heart disease.

Here are some statistics to think about. Drop in the risk of heart disease for every one percent decrease in blood cholesterol: 3–4 percent; blood cholesterol levels of vegetarians compared to nonvegetarians: 14 percent lower; risk of death from heart disease for vegetarians compared to nonvegetarians: one-half.

Cancer

We find further evidence in numerous studies establishing a relationship between colon cancer and meat-eating. Meat-centered diets are almost always high in fat and low in fiber, resulting in a slow transit time through the colon and allowing toxic wastes to do their damage. Peter R. Cheeke, professor of Animal Science at Oregon State University, writes, "Rates of colorectal cancer in various countries are strongly correlated with per capita consumption of red meat and animal fat, and inversely associated with fiber consumption. Even the most dedicated Animal Scientist or meat supporter must be somewhat dismayed by the preponderance of evidence suggesting a role of meat consumption in the etiology of colon cancer." Moreover, while being digested, meat is known to generate steroid metabolites possessing carcinogenic properties.

As mentioned previously, true carnivores move raw meat through their digestive tracts quickly – within about three hours. Humans, with their long digestive tracts, take between twelve and eighteen hours to process and digest flesh. Because the environment of the digestive tract is warm and moist, the meat rots and creates free radicals – unstable, destructive oxygen atoms that can cause cancer, premature aging, and other degenerative conditions. These free radicals are released into the body during the long digestion process.

As research continues, evidence linking meat-eating to other forms of cancer is building up at an alarming rate. William Castelli, MD, director of the Framingham Health Study and the National Heart, Lung, and Blood Institute, writes, "A low-fat plant-based diet would not only lower the heart attack rate about eighty-five percent, but would lower the cancer rate sixty percent."

Some of the most shocking results in cancer research have come from exploration of the effects of nitrosamines. Nitrosamines are formed when secondary amines, prevalent in beer, wine, tea, and tobacco, for example, react with chemical preservatives in meat. The Food and Drug Administration has labeled nitrosamines "one of the most formidable and versatile groups of carcinogens yet discovered, and their role ... in the etiology of human cancer has caused growing apprehension among experts." Dr. William Lijinsky of Oak Ridge National Laboratory conducted experiments in which nitrosamines were fed to test animals. Within six months he found malignant tumors in 100 percent of the animals. The cancers, he said, "are all over the place; in the brain, lungs, pancreas, stomach, liver, adrenals, and intestines. The animals are a bloody mess."

There are few current studies of the effects of nitrosamines on the human organism; that they are carcinogenic has long been proven. People who eat meat of any description are at risk.

Dangerous Chemicals in Meat

Numerous other potentially hazardous chemicals, of which consumers are generally unaware, are present in meat and meat products. In their book *Poisons in Your Body*, Gary and Steven

Null give us an inside look at the corporate-owned animal factory. "The animals are kept alive and fattened by the continuous administration of tranquilizers, hormones, antibiotics, and 2,700 other drugs," they write. "The process starts even before birth and continues long after death. Although these drugs will still be present in the meat when you eat it, the law does not require that they be listed on the package."

One of these chemicals is recombinant Bovine Growth Hormone (rBGH/BST), a synthetic growth hormone recently designed to replace diethylstilbestrol in the U.S., which was shown to be carcinogenic. rBGH/BST is used to increase milk production, despite the fact that the U.S. has a milk surplus. Aside from the fact that rBGH/BST treated milk has been banned as a serious health hazard by the members of the European Union and Canada, it has been linked to two much more serious health hazards for meat-eaters, because not only is the hormone present in the milk of treated cows and not removed by pasteurization, it is found in significant quantities in the meat.

The first is that cows treated with rBGH/BST tend to develop inflamed udders much more frequently than other cows. To counteract this problem, farmers pump their cows full of antibiotics, detectable residues of which remain in the cows' fatty tissues, including the fats in milk. This process is causing the growth of antibiotic-resistant bacteria, making antibiotics used to treat human disease less and less effective. The FDA estimates that penicillin and tetracycline save the meat industry $1.9 billion a year, giving them sufficient reason to overlook the potential health hazards to humans.

The second health hazard is the elevation of Insulin Growth Factor (IGF-1) found in hormone-treated milk. IGF-1 takes the same form in humans as it does in cows, and in both, controls the way the body's cells respond to growth hormones. An increase in IGF-1 in humans can cause a number of diseases, not the least of which are colorectal, thyroid, bone, epidermal, and breast cancer.

Mad Cow Disease

Formally known as bovine spongiform encephalopathy (BSE), mad cow disease has caused fear across the world. And so it should. But what causes it? BSE, scientists say, belongs to a family of brain-wasting diseases – other forms exist in sheep, mink, deer and elk, cats, and humans. Actually, it was the human form of the disease that helped researcher Stanley Pruisner, a biochemist at the University of California, find the source of the infection in the expression of a "prion," a piece of a protein. The disease, it was proven, was transmitted by cannibalism, as was the case with the human form of the disease – and *could* jump species, say, from infected beef to human.

Modern farmers around the world raise livestock in feedlots and feed them grain instead of grass. Grain is an expensive protein to grow, and farmers decided to take advantage of a cheaper source. Farm animals that die of disease, all the animal parts not used in the meat-packing and leather industries (up to one-half of an animal's weight), road kill, euthanized pets, and animal control kills are part of a 2.4-billion-dollar rendering industry. In Los Angeles alone, 200 tons of euthanized pets are sent every month to the renderers. The number is almost the same in the UK. All these animals and animal parts are steam-cooked until they separate into fats and protein solids. The fats are used for cosmetics, lubricants, soaps, and candles, and the protein solids are dried, pulverized, and sold as "protein concentrates" to feedlots. There, they are added to the animals' feed. Cows, sheep, chickens, and pigs are being forced to cannibalize their own kind.

In 1988, over 2,000 cases of BSE were reported in Great Britain. Despite a ban on feeding ruminant proteins to ruminants, 35,000 new cases of BSE were confirmed in 1992. In 1993, two British dairy farmers died of Creutzfeldt-Jakob disease (CJD), the human form of BSE. Two things became clear: BSE is transmitted from cow to calf through the milk, and other species can contract it by eating infected meat.

Great Britain is not alone either in its feedlot practices or in its dangers from BSE. American cows have had BSE, and American people have suffered from CJD. In April of 1996 eight cases of CJD were diagnosed in the northeastern corner of Texas alone. The normal rate of infection prior to BSE's jumping species is one death per million population.

And while both the U.S. and the United Kingdom have restricted farmers from feeding their livestock ruminant proteins, farmers have not given up on trying to provide their herbivorous animals with animal protein: spray-dried blood products, which have undergone little processing to remove infectivity, are being increasingly used in feed.

As of this writing (2006), new cases of BSE continue to break out in the U.S., England, Scotland, Sweden, Canada, and Japan. The danger is not over and the problem not solved.

Other Dangers

Sodium nitrate and sodium nitrite, chemicals used as preservatives to slow putrefaction in cured meat and meat products, including ham, bacon, bologna, salami, frankfurters, and fish, also endanger health. These chemicals give meat its bright red appearance by reacting with pigments in the blood and muscle. Without them, the natural gray-brown color of dead meat would turn away many prospective consumers.

Unfortunately, these chemicals do not distinguish between the blood of a corpse and the blood of a living human, and many persons accidentally subjected to excessive amounts have died of poisoning. Even smaller quantities can prove hazardous, especially for young children or babies, and therefore the United Nations' joint FAO/WHO Expert Committee on Food Additives has warned, "Nitrates should on no account be added to baby food." A. J. Lehman of the FDA pointed out that "only a small margin of safety exists between the amount of nitrate that is safe and that which may be dangerous."

The trauma of being slaughtered also adds "pain poisons" (powerful stimulants) into the meat. These join with unelimi-nated wastes in the animal's blood, such as urea and uric acid, to further contaminate the flesh consumers eat.

Diseases in Meat

In addition to dangerous chemicals, meat often carries diseases from the animals themselves. Crammed together in unclean conditions, force-fed, and inhumanely treated, animals des-tined for slaughter contract many more diseases than they would under normal conditions. Meat inspectors attempt to filter out unacceptable meats, but because of pressures from the industry and lack of sufficient time for examination (most inspections last under two minutes), much of what passes is far less wholesome than the meat purchaser realizes.

The USDA meat-inspection methods are questionable in any case. They are based on the Meat Inspection Act of 1907, which instructs inspectors to rely on sight, smell, and touch – the "poke and sniff" method – to check for contaminations. The problem is, however, that the "poke and sniff" method cannot detect such deadly contaminants as E. coli 0157:H7 or salmonella. In 1996, the USDA changed its inspection policy, allowing meat-packing companies to perform more of their own food inspections, resulting in even less concern for consumer safety.

And the USDA has been found lax in enforcing even these low standards. In its capacity of overseeing federal regulatory agencies, the U.S. General Accounting Office cited the USDA for failure to correct various violations by slaughterhouses. Carcasses contaminated with rodent feces, cockroaches, and rust were found in meat-packing companies such as Swift, Armour, and Carnation. Felicia Nestor, food safety director for the Government Accountability Project, told reporters, "Federal inspectors check paperwork, not food, and are prohibited from removing feces and other contaminants before products are stamped with the purple USDA seal of approval." Some 206 meat inspectors who responded to a 2004 survey said that "there were weekly or monthly instances when they did not take direct action against animal feces, vomit, metal shards, or other contamination because of the new USDA rules." Some inspectors rationalize the laxity, explaining that if regulations were enforced, no meat-packers would remain open for business.

It has also become common knowledge that seafood is contaminated by high levels of polychlorinated biphenyls (PCBs), caused by industrial waste run-off and dumping in our water systems. Some PCBs have dioxin-like properties (dioxin is one of the most toxic manmade chemicals), some act like hormones, and others function as nerve poisons. They cause cancer, liver disease, birth defects, and other serious diseases.

Pesticide Contamination

The majority of crops grown in the Western world are grown as cattle feed. Crops grown for animals are permitted to have much higher pesticide levels than crops grown for direct human consumption. The four constituents of cattle feed are corn, soybeans, cotton, and wheat, and when these crops are sprayed with heavy doses of pesticides and then eaten by livestock, carcinogenic chemical residues are stored in their tissues. Later, when the animals are slaughtered and unused portions of their bodies are rendered, the concentrates are added to animal feed. The chemical residues, already concentrated, become that much more concentrated, and are then passed on for human consumption. In her *Silent Spring,* published in 1962, Rachel Carson states that 637,666,000 pounds of synthetic poisons were being produced in the form of pesticides and herbicides each year for use in agriculture – mainly in livestock crops. By 1998, that number had increased by 400 percent, and today by 600 percent.

Nutrition Without Meat

Announcing that one is a vegetarian almost always elicits a predictable question: "What about protein?" To this a vegetarian might well reply, "What about the elephant? The bull? The rhinoceros?" The ideas that meat has a monopoly on protein and even that large amounts of protein are required for energy and strength are myths.

During digestion, most protein breaks down into its constituent amino acids, which are then used by the body for growth and tissue replacement. Of the twenty-two amino acids, the body can synthesize all but eight. These eight "essential" amino acids exist in abundance in nonflesh foods. Dairy products, grains, beans, and nuts are all concentrated sources of protein. Cheese, peanuts, and lentils, for instance, contain more protein per ounce than hamburger, pork, or porterhouse steak. A study by Dr. Fred Stare of Harvard and Dr. Mervyn Hoarding of Loma Linda University made extensive comparisons between the protein intake of vegetarians and that of flesh-eaters. They concluded that "each group exceeded twice its requirement for every essential amino acid and surpassed this amount by large margins for most of them."

For many Americans and Europeans, protein makes up more than 20 percent of their diet, nearly twice the quantity recommended by the World Health Organization. Although inadequate amounts of protein will cause loss of strength, the body cannot use excess protein; rather, it is converted into nitrogenous wastes that burden the kidneys and is eventually passed from the body, taking calcium with it. A number of studies have now linked the overeating of protein to the rise in osteoporosis. Although scientists have long known that osteoporosis results from reduced calcium in the bones, they are now coming to understand that one of the main causes of this deficiency is too much protein in the diet.

Carbohydrates are the body's primary energy source. Only as a last resort does the body use protein to produce energy.

Too much protein intake actually reduces the body's energy capacity. In a series of comparative endurance tests conducted by Dr. Irving Fisher of Yale, vegetarians performed twice as well as meat-eaters. By reducing the nonvegetarians' protein consumption by 20 percent, Dr. Fisher found their efficiency increased by 33 percent. Numerous other studies have shown that a proper vegetarian diet provides more nutritional energy than meat. Furthermore, a study by Dr. J. Iotekyo and V. Kipani at Brussels University showed that vegetarians were able to perform physical tests two to three times longer than meat-eaters before exhaustion, and were fully recovered from fatigue in one-fifth the time needed by meat-eaters.

2

The Hidden Cost of Meat: The Myth of Scarcity

"A reduction in beef and other meat consumption is the most potent single act you can take to halt the destruction of our environment and preserve our natural resources. Our choices do matter. What's healthiest for each of us personally is also healthiest for the life support system of our precious, but wounded, planet."

— John Robbins, author of *Diet for a New America* and president of the EarthSave Foundation, Santa Cruz, California

Solving the Hunger Problem

Food expert Francis Moore Lappé, author of the best-selling *Diet for a Small Planet*, once said in a television interview that we should look at a piece of steak as if it were a Cadillac. "What I mean," she explained, "is that we in America are hooked on gas-guzzling automobiles because of the illusion of cheap petroleum. Likewise, we got hooked on a grain-fed, meat-centered diet because of the illusion of cheap grain."

According to information compiled by the United States Department of Agriculture, over 90 percent of all the grain produced in America is used to feed livestock – cows, pigs, lambs, and chickens – animals that wind up on dinner tables.

Yet the process of using grain to produce meat is incredibly wasteful: the USDA's Economic Research Service shows that we get back only one pound of beef for every sixteen pounds of grain.

And as the world continues to pollute its natural resources, there's another significant concern in the raising of livestock: water. According to soil and water specialists at the University of California's Agricultural Extension, it takes 5,214 gallons of water to produce one pound of beef, 815 gallons of water to produce a pound of chicken, 1,630 gallons to produce a pound of pork, but only 23 gallons to produce a pound of lettuce and 25 gallons to produce a pound of wheat. Author and activist John Robbins writes, "In California today, you may save more water by not eating a pound of beef than you would by not showering for six entire months."

In his book *Proteins: Their Chemistry and Politics*, Dr. Aaron Altshul notes that in terms of calorie units per acre, a diet of grains, vegetables, and beans will support twenty times more people than a diet of meat. As it stands now, about half the harvested acreage in America and in a number of European, African, and Asian countries is used to feed animals. If the earth's arable land were used primarily for the production of vegetarian foods, the planet could easily support a human population of twenty billion and more.

Facts such as these have led food experts to point out that the world hunger problem is largely illusory. Even now, we are producing enough food for everyone on the planet. Unfortunately, it is being allocated inefficiently. The Global Hunger Alliance writes, "Most hunger deaths are due to chronic malnutrition caused by inequitable distribution and inefficient use of existing food resources. At the same time, wasteful agricultural practices, such as the intensive livestock operations known as factory farming, are rapidly polluting and depleting the natural resources upon which all life depends. Trying to produce more food by these methods would lead only to more water pollution, more soil degradation, and, ultimately, more hunger." A report submitted to the United Nations World Food Conference concurs: "The overconsumption of meat by the rich means hunger for the poor. This wasteful agriculture must be changed – by the suppression of feedlots where beef are fattened on grains, and even a massive reduction of beef cattle."

Living Cows Are an Economic Asset

It is quite clear that a living cow yields society more food than a dead one in the form of a continuing supply of milk, cheese, butter, yogurt, and other high-protein foods. In trying to solve the third-world hunger crisis, people have looked at countries like India and wondered why the people allow themselves to compete with cows for precious grain. Why don't they simply eat the cows? But most Hindus consider cows sacred and do not slaughter them. Because of this cultural bent, food ecologists have studied the symbiosis between humans and cows and tried to understand whether the relationship is actually competitive, and whether the hunger problem can be solved by slaughtering the cows. In a detailed study of cows in West Bengal, Stewart Odend'hal of the University of Missouri found that far from depriving humans of food, cows ate only inedible remains of harvested crops (rice hulls, tops of sugarcane, etc.) and grass. "Basically," he said, "the cattle convert items of little direct human value into products of immediate utility." This should put to rest the myth that people are starving in India because they will not kill their cows. Rather, studies show that the food problem in India has more to do with occasional severe drought, political upheaval, or industrialization than with cows. This is true in a number of third-world countries.

If allowed to live, cows produce high quality, protein-rich foods in amounts that stagger the imagination. In the 80s in America, there was a deliberate attempt to limit dairy production, and the government was forced to stockpile butter, cheese, and nonfat dried milk. The supply grew by about 45 million pounds each week. In fact, the 10 million cows in America at that time provided so much milk that the government periodically released millions of pounds of dairy products for free distribution to the poor and hungry. It's abundantly clear that cows (living ones) are one of mankind's most valuable food resources. Sadly, in the mid-'80s the U.S. government bought and slaughtered millions of dairy cows to end the need to support milk prices by stockpiling dairy products.

Movements to save seals, dolphins, and whales from slaughter are flourishing, so why shouldn't there be a movement to save cows? From the economic standpoint alone it seems like a sound idea.

You're Paying More for Meat than You Think

The meat industry is a powerful economic and political force, and besides spending millions of its own dollars to promote meat-eating, it has also managed to grab an unfair share of our tax dollars. Practically speaking, the meat production process is so wasteful and costly that the industry must be subsidized to survive. Most people are unaware of how heavily national governments support the meat industry with outright grants, favorable loan guarantees, and purchases of its surplus products, which are often destroyed. The price tag of those government subsidies shows up in the health of our children. In 2003, the U.S.'s National School Lunch Program gave schools more than 6 billion dollars to offer low-cost meals to students. That sounds like charity, but the National School Lunch Program was originally designed to serve two purposes: to provide healthy meals to children regardless of income, and to subsidize agribusiness by "shoring up demand for beef." In light of all the health hazards of a meat-based diet, what is this doing to our children, and to families who have little choice but to accept the subsidized lunches?

These days, the federal government purchases more than $800 million worth of mostly meat and dairy products each year and delivers them to schools to serve to their students. Although the federal government is supposed to purchase all farm products – grains, vegetables, and fruits, as well as meat and dairy – it tends to make its purchases in direct response to lobbying. In 2001, the USDA spent a total of $350 million on surplus beef and other meat products for schools – more than double what it spent on fruits and vegetables (most of which were canned or frozen). Jennifer Raymond, a nutritionist who has worked with schools to develop healthier menus, states, "Basically, it's a welfare program for suppliers ... It's a price support program for agricultural producers, and the schools are simply a way to get rid of the items that have been purchased." The money to run this "welfare program" comes out of tax dollars. And citizens are also left with their children's health bill, as parents now battle such previously rare problems as childhood obesity, heart disease, Type II diabetes, and all the other once adult problems that go along with a high-cholesterol, high-saturated-fat diet.

More tax dollars go down the drain in the form of the millions of dollars the U.S. government spends each year to maintain a nationwide network of inspectors to monitor the little-publicized problem of animal diseases. When diseased animals are destroyed, the government pays the owners an indemnity. A *New York Times* editorial called this subsidy bill "outrageous," characterizing it as "a scandalous steal out of the public treasury." Nowadays, governments around the developed world pay farmers for their "mad cows." In 2001 alone, the UK government paid out over 91 million pounds sterling for "mad cows," and other governments have had similar bills.

Environmental Damage

Another price we pay for meat-eating is degradation of the environment. The United States Agricultural Research Service calls the heavily contaminated runoff and sewage from America's thousands of slaughterhouses and feedlots a major source of pollution of the nation's rivers and streams. It is fast becoming apparent that the freshwater resources of this planet are not only becoming polluted but depleted. The meat industry is particularly wasteful.

John Robbins, in his book *The Food Revolution*, writes, "There are more chickens processed annually in the United States than there are people in the world – 7.6 billion chickens versus 6 billion humans. There are more turkeys in the United States than there are *Homo sapiens* – 300 million of the big birds versus 280 million of us. Plus there are now about 100 million hogs and 60 million beef cattle in the United States. What do you think happens to the excrement from so many animals?" Who thinks about it?

Although manure has always been a natural fertilizer, the sheer mountains of the stuff have become a real disposal problem. Unfortunately, much of it ends up in our waterways. "Mass production of meat has become a staggering source of pollution.... In recent years livestock waste has been implicated in massive fish kills and outbreaks of such diseases as pfiesteria, which causes memory loss, confusion and acute skin burning in people exposed to contaminated water. In the United States, livestock now produces 130 times as much waste as people do.... These mega-farms are proliferating, and in populous areas their waste is tainting drinking water." (*Time*, November 8, 1999)

Global Warming

The atmosphere is composed of a mixture of gases, the exact constituents of which have remained stable for eons. But as the twentieth century has moved into the twenty-first, we are facing a crisis of epic proportions. Nature has maintained a delicate balance of oxygen and carbon dioxide in our atmosphere. With the current increase in carbon dioxide, we're seeing the results: the polar ice caps are beginning to melt, sea levels are rising, and climate changes are obvious the world over.

The culprit most usually cited for global warming is our burning of such large quantities of fossil fuels. Emissions are heaviest, of course, in the industrialized world. A significant contributor to these emissions is the agricultural industry, mainly due to the use of large amounts of nitrogen fertilizers. Ammonium nitrate, the most common form of nitrogen fertilizer, is actually derived from natural gas, a fossil fuel. One quarter of the nitrogen fertilizer used in the United States is used on corn grown as livestock feed.

Although the United States government has tried to minimize the importance of global warming, climate change has serious consequences for every species of life. Conservative estimates tell us that the earth's temperature may rise by four degrees over the next century. Environmentalist David Suzuki writes, "[M]ost of us can adapt to one degree [of change]. But four degrees is virtually the difference between an ice age and a warm epoch like we're in now. It takes nature ten thousand years to make those kinds of changes, and we're talking about changes like that on the order of a century. There isn't an ecologist anywhere who thinks that we can adapt to that without dramatic dislocation to the species in the world, and to agriculture and other patterns of living that depend on climate." The Western world's unparalleled meat-eating is contributing significantly to this climate change.

Social Conflict

The wasteful process of meat production, which requires far larger acreages of land than vegetable agriculture, has been a source of economic conflict in human society for thousands of years. A study published in *Plant Foods for Human Nutrition* reveals that an acre of grain produces five times more protein than an acre of pasture set aside for meat production. An acre of beans or peas produces ten times more, and an acre of spinach twenty-eight times more protein. Economic facts like these were known even to the ancient Greeks. In Plato's *Republic*, the great Greek philosopher Socrates recommended a vegetarian diet because it would allow a country to make the most intelligent use of its agricultural resources. He warned that if people began eating animals, there would be need for more pasturing land. "'And the country which was enough to support the original inhabitants will be too small now, and not enough?' he asked Glaucon, who replied that this was indeed true. 'And so we shall go to war, Glaucon, shall we not?' To which Glaucon replied, 'Most certainly.'"

It is interesting to note that meat-eating played a role in many of the wars during the age of European colonial expansion. The spice trade with India and other countries of the East was a source of great contention. Europeans subsisted on a diet of meat preserved with salt. In order to disguise and vary the monotonous and unpleasant taste of their food, they eagerly purchased vast quantities of spices. So huge were the fortunes

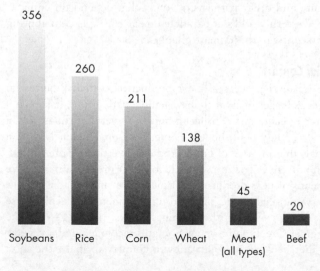

Relative Per-Acre Yields of Usable Protein from Various Food Sources

Soybeans	Rice	Corn	Wheat	Meat (all types)	Beef
356	260	211	138	45	20

to be made in the spice trade that governments and merchants did not hesitate to use arms to secure sources.

Even in the present era much of the world's mass conflict is centered on food shortages. As far back as 1974, the U.S.'s Central Intelligence Agency (CIA) published a report warning that in the near future there may not be enough food for the world's population "unless the affluent nations make a quick and drastic cut in their consumption of grain-fed animals." Things have not improved.

Meat-eating in industrialized nations is certainly linked to world hunger – and therefore to war, which in turn causes more hunger. Forty thousand children around the world die each day from malnutrition. U.S. livestock eats enough grain and soybeans each year to feed more than five times the entire U.S. population. According to one study, if Americans reduced their meat consumption by only 10 percent, 12 million tons of grain would be freed up annually for human consumption – enough to feed each of the 60 million children and adults who starve to death each year.

Saving Money with a Vegetarian Diet
But now let's turn from the geopolitical situation and get down to our own pocketbooks. Although not widely known fact, grains, beans, and milk products are an excellent source of high-quality protein. Pound for pound, many vegetarian foods are better sources of this essential nutrient than meat. A hundred-gram portion of meat contains only twenty grams of protein. (Another fact to consider: meat is more than 50 percent water by weight.) In comparison, a 100-gram portion of cheese or lentils yields twenty-five grams of protein, while a hundred grams of soybeans yields thirty-four grams of protein. But although meat provides less protein, it costs much more. A spot check of supermarkets in Florida in August 2005 showed sirloin steak costing $7.89 a pound, while staple ingredients for delicious vegetarian meals averaged less than $1.50 a pound.

An eight-ounce container of cottage cheese costing $1.59 provides 60 percent of the minimum daily requirement of protein. Becoming a vegetarian could potentially save an individual shopper at least several hundred dollars each year, thousands of dollars over the course of a lifetime. The savings to consumers as a whole would amount to billions of dollars annually. Considering all this, it's hard to see how anyone could afford *not* to become a vegetarian.

3

Factory Farming and Compassion

"If you could feel or see the suffering, you wouldn't think twice. Give back life. Don't eat meat."

— Kim Basinger

In 2003, just under 10 billion animals (excluding aquatics) were killed, according to data extrapolated from the USDA's National Agricultural Statistics Service (NASS). The NASS does not count aquatic animals, but estimates that the numbers of these animals killed exceeds the number of slaughtered land animals. The NASS also expected there to be a 2.5 percent increase in the number of animals killed in 2004. According to the Farm Animal Reform Movement (FARM), "of the 10.2 billion farmed animals expected to be killed this year [2004], 868 million (or 8.7%) will succumb to disease, malnutrition, injury, suffocation, stress, 'culling,' or other deadly factory farming practices before reaching the slaughterhouse. 'Layer' hens will experience the highest rate of non-slaughter death – a staggering 64.5% – primarily because all males are deliberately suffocated at birth.... Globally, the number of animals slaughtered for food in 2003 was 52.7 billion, according to the U.N. Food and Agriculture Organization. This conservative figure does not account for non-slaughter deaths, under-reporting by smaller countries, and many billions of aquatic animals."

These numbers are mind-boggling, but few people make any conscious connection between the slaughter and the meat products that appear on their dinner tables. A case in point: in television commercials, Ronald McDonald tells children that hamburgers grow in "hamburger patches." The truth is much less pleasant. Commercial slaughterhouses are visions of hell. Screaming animals are stunned by hammer blows, electric shock, or concussion guns. They are then hoisted alive into the air by the feet and moved through the factories of death on mechanized conveyor systems. Their throats are then cut and they are skinned alive. In the November/December 1999 issue of *Business Ethics*, this scene was described: "We must express concern about slaughterhouse cruelty by McDonald's suppliers.... [F]ederal standards require that 100 percent of cows be fully stunned before they are skinned, but [according to] ... a McDonald's training video ... it's acceptable if five cows in every 100 are conscious while skinned and dismembered.... And the real error rate may be far more than 5 percent." Describing his reaction to a visit to a slaughterhouse, champion tennis player Peter Burwash wrote in *A Vegetarian Primer*, "I'm no shrinking violet. I played hockey until half of my teeth were knocked down my throat. And I'm extremely competitive on a tennis court.... But that experience at the slaughterhouse overwhelmed me. When I walked out of there, I knew all the physiological, economic, and ecological arguments supporting vegetarianism, but it was firsthand experience of man's cruelty to animals that laid the real groundwork for my commitment to vegetarianism."

Ancient Greece and Rome

Ethical considerations have attracted many of the world's greatest personalities to adopt a vegetarian diet. Pythagoras, famous for his contributions to geometry and mathematics, said, "O my fellow men, do not defile your bodies with sinful foods. We have corn, we have apples bending down the branches with their weight, and grapes swelling on the vines. There are sweet-flavored herbs, and vegetables which can be cooked and soft-ened over the fire, nor are you denied milk or thyme-scented honey. The earth affords a lavish supply of riches, of innocent foods, and offers you banquets that involve no bloodshed or slaughter: only beasts satisfy their hunger with flesh, and not even all of those, because horses, cattle, and sheep live on grass." The biographer Diogenes tells us that Pythagoras ate bread and honey in the morning and raw vegetables at night. He would also pay fisherman to throw their catch back into the sea.

In an essay titled "On Eating Flesh," the Roman author Plutarch wrote: "Can you really ask what reason Pythagoras had for abstinence from flesh? For my part I rather wonder both by what accident and in what state of mind the first man touched his mouth to gore and brought his lips to the flesh of a dead creature, set forth tables of dead, stale bodies, and ventured to call food and nourishment the parts that has a little before bellowed and cried, moved and lived. How could eyes endure the slaughter when throats were slit and hides flayed and limbs torn from limb? How could his nose endure the stench? How was it that the pollution did not turn away his taste, which made contact with sores of others and sucked juices and serums from mortal wounds? It is certainly not lions or wolves that we eat out of self-defense; on the contrary, we ignore these and slaughter harmless, tame creatures without stings or teeth to harm us. For the sake of a little flesh we deprive them of sun, of light, of the duration of life to which they are entitled by birth and being."

He then delivered this challenge to flesh-eaters: "If you declare that you are naturally designed for such a diet, then first kill for yourself what you want to eat. Do it, however, only through your own resources, unaided by cleaver or cudgel or any kind of ax."

Da Vinci, Rousseau, Franklin...

The great Renaissance painter, inventor, sculptor, and poet Leonardo da Vinci epitomized the ethical approach to vegetarianism. He wrote, "He who does not value life does not deserve it." He considered the bodies of meat-eaters to be "burial places," graveyards for the animals they eat. His notebooks are full of passages that show his compassion for living creatures. He lamented, "Endless numbers of these animals shall have their little children taken from them, ripped open, and barbarously slaughtered."

French philosopher Jean Jacques Rousseau was an advocate of natural order. He observed that meat-eating animals are generally more cruel and violent than herbivores. He therefore reasoned that a vegetarian diet would produce a more compassionate person. He even advised that butchers not be allowed to testify in court or sit on juries.

In *The Wealth of Nations*, economist Adam Smith proclaimed the advantages of a vegetarian diet. "It may indeed be doubted whether butchers' meat is anywhere a necessary of life. Grain and other vegetables, with the help of milk, cheese, and butter, or oil, where butter is not to be had, afford the most plentiful, the most wholesome, the most nourishing, and the most invigorating diet. Decency nowhere requires that any man should eat butchers' meat." Similar considerations motivated Benjamin Franklin, who became a vegetarian at age sixteen. Franklin noted "greater progress, from that greater clearness of head and quicker apprehension." In his autobiographical writings, he called flesh-eating "unprovoked murder."

The poet Shelley was a committed vegetarian. In his essay "A Vindication of Natural Diet" he wrote, "Let the advocate of animal food force himself to a decisive experiment on its fitness, and as Plutarch recommends, tear a living lamb with his teeth and, plunging his head into its vitals, slake his thirst with the steaming blood.... Then, and then only, would he be consistent." Shelley's interest in vegetarianism began when he was a student at Oxford, and he and his wife Harriet took up the diet soon after their marriage. In a letter dated March 14, 1812, his wife wrote to a friend, "We have foresworn meat and adopted the Pythagorean system." Shelley, in his poem "Queen Mab," described a utopian world where men do not kill animals for food.

> ... no longer now
> He slays the lamb that looks him in the face,
> And horribly devours his mangled flesh,
> Which, still avenging Nature's broken law,
> Kindled all putrid humors in his frame,
> All evil passions, and all vain belief,
> Hatred, despair, and loathing in his mind,
> The germs of misery, death, disease and crime.

The Russian author Leo Tolstoy became a vegetarian in 1885. Giving up the sport of hunting, he advocated "vegetarian pacifism" and was against killing even the smallest living things, such as ants. He felt there was a natural progression of violence that led inevitably to war in human society. In his essay "The First Step," Tolstoy wrote that flesh-eating is "simply immoral, as it involves the performance of an act which is contrary to moral feeling – killing." By killing, Tolstoy believed, "man suppresses in himself, unnecessarily, the highest spiritual capacity – that of sympathy and pity towards living creatures like himself – and by violating his own feelings becomes cruel."

Composer Richard Wagner believed that all life was sacred. He saw vegetarianism as "nature's diet," which could save humankind from violent tendencies and help us return to the "long-lost Paradise."

At various times in his life, Henry David Thoreau was a vegetarian. Although his own practice of vegetarianism was spotty at best, he recognized its virtues. In Walden he wrote, "Is it not a reproach that man is a carnivorous animal? True, he can and does live, in a great measure, by preying on other animals; but this is a miserable way – as anyone who will go to snaring rabbits, or slaughtering lambs, may learn – and he will be regarded as a benefactor of his race who shall teach man to confine himself to a more innocent and wholesome diet. Whatever my own practice may be, I have no doubt that it is a part of the destiny of the human race, in its gradual improvement, to leave off eating animals, as surely as the savage tribes have left off eating each other when they came in contact with the more civilized."

The Twentieth Century

It goes without saying that the great twentieth-century apostle of nonviolence Mahatma Gandhi was a vegetarian. His parents, being devout Hindus, never gave him meat, fish, or eggs. Under British rule, however, there was an attack on the age-old principles of Indian culture. Under such pressure, many Indians adopted the meat-eating habits of the West. Even Gandhi fell victim to the advice of school friends, who urged him to eat meat to increase his strength and courage. He later resumed a vegetarian diet and wrote, "It is necessary to correct the error that vegetarianism has made us weak in mind, or passive or inert in action. I do not regard flesh-food as necessary at any stage." Gandhi wrote several books in which he discussed vegetarianism. His own daily diet included wheat sprouts, almond paste, greens, lemons, and honey. He founded Tolstoy Farm, a community based on vegetarian principles. In his *Moral Basis of Vegetarianism* Gandhi wrote, "I hold flesh-food to be unsuited to our species. We err in copying the lower animal world if we are superior to it." He felt that ethical principles are a stronger support for a lifelong commitment to a vegetarian diet than reasons of health. "I so feel," he stated, "that spiritual progress does demand at some stage that we should cease to kill our fellow creatures for the satisfaction of our bodily wants."

Playwright George Bernard Shaw first became a vegetarian at age twenty-five. "It was Shelley who first opened my eyes to the savagery of my diet," he wrote in his autobiography. Shaw's doctors warned that the diet would kill him. When an old man, he was asked why he didn't go back and show them what good it had done him. He replied, "I would, but they all passed away years ago." Once someone asked him how it was that he looked so youthful. "I don't," Shaw retorted. "I look my age. It is the other people who look older than they are. What can you expect from people who eat corpses?" On the connection between flesh-eating and violence in human society, Shaw wrote:

> We pray on Sundays that we may have light
>   To guide our footsteps on the path we tread;
> We are sick of war, we don't want to fight,
>   And yet we gorge ourselves upon the dead.

H. G. Wells wrote about vegetarianism in his vision of a future world, *A Modern Utopia*: "In all the round world of Utopia there is no meat. There used to be. But now we cannot stand the thought of slaughterhouses. And, in a population that is all educated, and at about the same level of physical refinement, it is practically impossible to find anyone who will hew a dead ox or pig....I can still remember as a boy the rejoicings over the closing of the last slaughterhouse."

Nobel Prize–winning author Isaac Bashevis Singer became a vegetarian in 1962, at the age of fifty-eight. He said, "Naturally I am sorry now that I waited so long, but it is better later than never." He found vegetarianism quite compatible with his mystical variety of Judaism. "We are all God's creatures – that we pray to God for mercy and justice while we continue to eat the flesh of animals that are slaughtered on our account is not consistent." Although he appreciates the health aspect of vegetarianism, he states very clearly that the ethical consideration is primary. "Even if eating flesh was actually shown to be good for you, I would certainly still not eat it."

Singer has little patience with intellectual rationalizations for meat-eating. "Various philosophers and religious leaders tried to convince their disciples and followers that animals are nothing more than machines without a soul, without feelings. However, anyone who has ever lived with an animal – be it a dog, a bird, or even a mouse – knows that this theory is a brazen lie, invented to justify cruelty."

A world of authors, philosophers, and scientists – including Sir Isaac Newton, Albert Einstein, St. Francis of Assisi, George Bernard Shaw, Mark Twain, and Alice Walker – are or were vegetarians. Nowadays there are countless celebrities – actors, writers, athletes, thinkers – who have embraced the ecological sanity and compassion of the vegetarian diet. A number of these people have been outspoken about their choice to renounce meat as a food. Among celebrity vegetarians are film stars Orlando Bloom, Liv Tyler, Brad Pitt, Richard Gere, Jude Law, Josh Hartnett, Gwyneth Paltrow, Steve Martin, Alec Baldwin, Drew Barrymore, Ryan Gosling, Kim Basinger, and Dustin Hoffman; recording artists Dr. Dre, the B52s, Paul and the late Linda McCartney, Chrissie Hynde, Joaquin Phoenix, Andre3000, Meatloaf, Peter Gabriel, K. D. Lang, Elvis Costello, and Melissa Etheridge; models Brooke Shields, Christy Turlington, Cindy Jackson, and Christie Brinkley; sports stars Hank Aaron (baseball champion), B. J. Armstrong (basketball star), Andreas Cahling (bodybuilder), Sally Eastall (marathon runner), Sylvia Cranston (triathlete), Chris Campbell (world wrestling champion), Aaron Pryor (welterweight world boxing champion), Edward Moses (world record holder for the 400-meter hurdles), Robert de Castella (Olympic marathon champion), Anton Innauer (Olympic ski champion), and Killer Kowalski (wrestler).

Vegetarianism and Religion

Avoidance of meat has been a part of religious practice in nearly all faiths. Some Egyptian priests were vegetarians, avoiding meat in order to help them maintain vows of celibacy. They also avoided eggs, which they called "liquid flesh."

Although the Old Testament, the foundation of Judaism, contains prescriptions for meat-eating, it is clear that the ideal situation is vegetarianism. In Genesis (1:29) we find God Himself proclaiming: "Behold, I have given you every seed-yielding plant that is on the surface of all the earth, and every tree which has fruit yielding seed; it shall be food for you." In the beginning of creation as described in the Bible, it seems that not even the animals ate flesh. In Genesis (1:30) God says, "And to every beast of the earth, and to every fowl of the air, and to every thing that creepeth upon the earth, wherein there is life, I have given every green herb for meat; and it was so." Genesis (9:4–5) also directly forbids meat eating: "But flesh with the life thereof, which is the blood thereof, shall ye not eat."

In the Bible we also find the story of Daniel, who while imprisoned in Babylon refused to eat the meat offered by his jailers, preferring instead simple vegetarian food.

Major stumbling blocks for many Christians are the belief that Christ ate meat and the many references to meat in the New Testament. But close study of the original Greek manuscripts shows that the vast majority of the words translated as "meat" are *trophe*, *brome*, and other words that simply mean "food" or "eating" in the broadest sense. For example, in the Gospel of St. Luke (8:55), we read that Jesus raised a woman from the dead and "commanded to give her meat." The original Greek word translated as "meat" is *phago*, which simply means "to eat." What Christ actually said was "Let her eat." The Greek word for meat is *kreas* ("flesh"), and it is never used in connection with Christ.

Nowhere in the New Testament is there any direct reference to Jesus eating meat. This is in line with Isaiah's famous prophecy about Jesus's appearance: "Behold, a virgin shall conceive, and bear a son, and shall call his name Immanuel. Butter and honey shall he eat, that he may know to refuse the evil and choose the good."

Clement of Alexandria, an early Church father, recommended a fleshless diet, citing the example of the apostle Matthew, who "partook of seeds, and nuts, and vegetables, without flesh." St. Jerome, another leader of the early Christian Church, who gave the authorized Latin version of the Bible still in use today, wrote, "The preparation of vegetables, fruit, and pulse is easy, and does not require expensive cooks." He felt such a diet was the best for a life devoted to the pursuit of wisdom. St. John Chrysostom considered meat-eating to be a cruel and unnatural habit for Christians. "We imitate but the ways of wolves, but the ways of leopards, or rather we are even worse than these. For to them nature has assigned that they should be thus fed, but us God hath honored with speech and a sense of equity, and we have become worse than the wild beasts." St. Benedict, who founded the Benedictine Order in A.D. 529, stipulated vegetable foods as the staple for his monks. The Trappist order uniformly prohibited meat, eggs, and other flesh foods from its founding in the seventeenth century. The regulations were relaxed by the Second Vatican Council in the 1960s, but most of the Trappists still follow the original teachings. Remarkably enough, however, many Trappist monasteries raise cattle for slaughter to support themselves financially.

The Seventh Day Adventist Church strongly recommends vegetarianism for its members. Although a fact little known to the general public, the huge American breakfast cereal industry got its start at an Adventist health resort run by Dr. John H. Kellogg. Dr. Kellogg was constantly devising new varieties of vegetarian breakfast foods for the wealthy patients of his Battle Creek Sanitorium. One of his inventions was "corn flakes," which he later marketed nationwide. Over the course of time, he gradually separated his business from the Seventh Day Adventist Church and formed the company that still bears his name.

The largest concentration of vegetarians in the world is found in India, the homeland of Buddhism and Hinduism. Buddhism began as a reaction to the widespread animal slaughter that was being carried out through perversion of religious rituals. Buddha put an end to these practices by propounding his doctrine of *ahimsa*, or nonviolence.

Indian Philosophy and Nonviolence

The Vedic scriptures of India, which predate Buddhism, also stress nonviolence as the ethical foundation of vegetarianism. The *Manu-samhitā*, the ancient Indian code of law, states, "Meat can never be obtained without injury to living creatures, and injury to sentient beings is detrimental to the attainment of heavenly bliss; let him therefore shun the use of meat." In another section, the *Manu-samhitā* warns, "Having well considered the disgusting origin of flesh and the cruelty of fettering and slaying of corporeal beings, let him entirely abstain from eating flesh."

In recent years the Hare Krishna movement has introduced these ethical considerations around the world. Śrīla Prabhupāda, the movement's founder-*ācārya* (spiritual master), once stated, "In the *Manu-samhitā* the concept of a life for a life is sanctioned, and it is actually observed throughout the world. Similarly, there are other laws which state that one cannot even kill an ant without being responsible. Since we cannot create, we have no right to kill any living entity, and therefore man-made laws that distinguish between killing a man and killing an animal are imperfect.... According to the laws of God, killing an animal is as punishable as killing a man. Those who draw distinctions between the two are concocting their own laws. Even in the Ten Commandments it is prescribed, 'Thou shalt not kill.' This is a perfect law, but by discriminating and speculating men distort it. 'I shall not kill man, but I shall kill animals.' In this way people cheat themselves and inflict suffering on themselves and others."

Emphasizing the Vedic conception of the unity of all life, Śrīla Prabhupāda then stated, "Everyone is God's creature, although in different bodies or dresses. God is considered the one supreme father. A father may have many children, and some may be intelligent and others not very intelligent, but if an intelligent son tells his father, 'My brother is not very intelligent; let me kill him,' will the father agree? ... Similarly, if God is the supreme father, why should He sanction the killing of animals, who are also His sons?"

4

Karma and Reincarnation

"In human society, if one kills a man he has to be hanged. That is the law of the state. Because of ignorance people do not perceive that there is a complete state controlled by the Supreme Lord. Every living creature is the son of the Supreme Lord, and He does not tolerate even an ant's being killed. One has to pay for it."

— Śrīla Prabhupāda

Capital punishment is the state's ultimate act of reprisal, and no sacrifice surpasses offering one's life for the sake of others. But although we seemingly attach great value to life, each year in the world billions of defenseless animals are butchered. This wholesale slaughter of animals is not necessary to prevent us from starving. Moreover, it is economically extravagant, environmentally damaging, and ethically reprehensible. Most seriously, however, animal killing violates the universal law of karma, which is similar to the modern scientific principle of action and reaction.

Scientists clearly understand how the physical law of action and reaction ("for every action there is an equal and opposite reaction") applies to material objects, but most are unaware of the more subtle laws of action and reaction in the realm of consciousness. Nevertheless, we do have a kind of instinctive awareness that somehow we all create our own happiness and distress. This realization dawns on us when in response to some mishap we reflect, "Well, maybe I had that coming."

In fact, we sometimes find people jokingly attributing unfortunate occurrences in their lives to "bad karma." But the law of karma insures that those who cause violence and suffering to other living beings must themselves experience equivalent violence and suffering – immediately or in the future. It's how the universe stays balanced.

Karma, as many in the West now know, is intimately related with the principle of reincarnation. In India's greatest spiritual classic, *Bhagavad-gītā*, Lord Kṛṣṇa describes the soul as the source of consciousness and the active principle that animates the body of every living being. This vital force, which is of the same spiritual quality in all beings, is distinct from and superior to the matter comprising the temporary material form. At the time of death, the indestructible soul transmigrates into another physical body, just as one changes clothing. All living beings (not just a few select individuals) undergo this process of reincarnation lifetime after lifetime. The *Bhagavad-gītā* states, "As a person puts on new garments, giving up old ones, similarly, the soul accepts new material bodies, giving up the old and useless ones."

The Journey of the Soul

The *Vedas* explain that the soul, known as the *ātmā*, may inhabit any of 8,400,000 general species of material bodies. The physical forms vary in complexity, beginning with the primitive microbes and amoebas, continuing on through the aquatic, plant, insect, reptile, bird, and animal species, and culminating in human beings and demigods. In consequence of its own desires to enjoy matter, the *ātmā* continually journeys through these various bodies, on an endless voyage of births and deaths.

The action of the mind is the prime force compelling the

living entity to transmigrate from one body to another. The *Gītā* explains, "Whatever state of being one remembers when he quits his body, that state of being he will attain without fail." Our minds are constantly recording all our thoughts and desires, and the totality of these memories floods our consciousness in the last moments of life. The nature of our thoughts at this critical juncture propels us into the appropriate physical body. Thus the body we now occupy is an accurate physical projection of our state of mind at the time of our last death.

The *Bhagavad-gītā* explains, "The living entity, thus taking another gross body, obtains a certain type of eye, ear, tongue, nose, and sense of touch, which are grouped around the mind. He thus enjoys a particular set of sense objects."

According to the *Vedas*, a soul in a form lower than human automatically evolves to the next-higher species, ultimately arriving at the human form. But because the human being possesses freedom to choose between matter and spirit, there is a chance that the soul will descend again into the lower species. The laws of karma are so arranged that if a human lives and dies with the animalistic mentality of a creature such as a dog, then in the next life he will be able to fulfill his doglike desires through the senses and organs of a dog. This is certainly an unfortunate occurrence, but such a fate is a definite possibility for a person immersed in ignorance. The *Gītā* declares, "When he dies in the mode of ignorance, he takes birth in the animal kingdom."

So the soul in the body of an animal may once have inhabited a human form and vice versa. Although a soul may successively occupy plant, animal, and human bodies, its intrinsic nature remains the same. Because the soul is pure spiritual energy, it cannot be altered in any way by matter. The *Bhagavad-gītā* explains that the soul is immutable. It is only the bodily covering, with its particular combination of mind and senses, that temporarily restricts or releases the conscious energy of the soul.

The Equality of All Living Things

The basic and transcendental equality of all conscious entities is not an abstract notion but is obvious to everyday sense perception – if only we look beyond the superficial differences in the varieties of material bodies. Anyone who has ever had a pet or visited the zoo has experienced that animals behave much like humans as they search for food, protect their young, play, sleep, and fight. The outstanding difference is that their intelligence and emotions are less developed, but this distinction is insufficient to discount the far more numerous and significant similarities in thinking, feeling, and willing that clearly point toward the universal equality of the consciousness within all bodies.

In nonhuman species, the living being is stringently controlled by its natural instincts. It is deprived of freedom of choice in eating, sleeping, mating, and defending, being compelled by bodily demands to follow rigid behavioral patterns. For this reason, the *ātmā* dwelling in forms of life lower than human is not responsible for its actions and thus does not generate new karma. A similar principle operates in our everyday experience – a dog chasing a cat across the roadway is immune to traffic citations. Animals are not expected to understand or obey a sophisticated set of laws. On the other hand, in both the social order and the universal order, human beings are obligated to be both informed and obedient.

Therefore, when a human unnecessarily takes the life of another entity, especially while causing that entity great pain and suffering, this act of overt aggression produces a severe karmic reaction. And, if year after year millions of animals are mercilessly butchered in huge, mechanized slaughterhouses, the accumulated negative karma produced by all those participating is unfathomable.

In his *Bhagavad-gītā* commentary, Śrīla Prabhupāda sternly warns about the karmic danger of animal slaughter. "In human society, if one kills a man he has to be hanged. That is the law of the state. Because of ignorance people do not perceive that there is a complete state controlled by the Supreme Lord. Every living creature is the son of the Supreme Lord, and He does not tolerate even an ant's being killed. One has to pay for it."

"Do Unto Others..."

This same instruction is present in all religious teachings. The Bible emphatically states, "Thou shall not kill," and Lord Jesus Christ, who always displayed deep compassion for all living beings, stated, "Do unto others as you would have them do unto you." Lord Buddha taught the principle of *ahimsa*, non-violence, specifically to protect innocent creatures from being slaughtered.

People who find personally killing an animal too gruesome tend to believe that merely eating its flesh does not implicate them in the violence. But this opinion is shortsighted and unsupported by any valid spiritual authority. According to the law of karma, all those who are connected to the killing of an animal are liable – the person who gives permission for the killing, the person who kills, the person who helps, the person who purchases the meat, the person who cooks the flesh, and the person who eats it. (These six guilty parties are enumerated in the *Manu-samhita*, the aforementioned ancient lawbook of India.) In a court of law all those who conspire in a murder are considered responsible, especially the party who purchases the assassin's services.

Psychological and emotional growth are essential to a progressive life, and all our thoughts and actions influence our character development. The Bible explains, "As you sow, so shall you reap." And the subtle laws of karma inform us that negative personality traits such as hostility, cruelty, depression, arrogance, apathy, insensitivity, anxiety, and envy are the psychological harvest of those who directly or indirectly make killing a regular feature in their lives. When people adopt a vegetarian diet, it is much easier for them to remain peaceful, happy, productive, and concerned for the welfare of others. As Albert Einstein said, "The vegetarian manner of living, by its purely physical effect on the human temperament, would most beneficially influence the lot of mankind." But when human consciousness is polluted by the effects of the negative karma resulting from destructive and injurious actions, its good qualities become covered.

The Cause of Violence

At present, despite impressive advances in science and technology, the world is faced with a crisis of unremitting violence in the shape of war, terrorism, murder, vandalism, child abuse, and abortion. More than 140 wars have been fought since the United Nations was formed in 1945, and in America alone, over 20,000 people are murdered each year. With social and political solutions conspicuously failing, perhaps it's time to analyze the problem from a different perspective – the law of karma. The callous and brutal slaughter of countless helpless animals must be considered a powerful causative factor in this wave of uncheckable violence.

In his purports to *Śrīmad-Bhāgavatam*, Śrīla Prabhupāda has pointed out how widespread violence among humans is a karmic reaction to animal slaughter. "In this age the propensity for mercy is almost nil. Consequently there is always fighting and war between men and nations. Men do not understand that because they unrestrictedly kill so many animals, they must also be slaughtered like animals in big wars. This is very much evident in the Western countries. In the West, slaughterhouses are maintained without restriction, and therefore every fifth or tenth year there is a big war in which countless people are slaughtered even more cruelly than the animals. Sometimes during war, soldiers keep their enemies in concentration camps and kill them in very cruel ways. These are reactions brought about by unrestricted animal-killing in the slaughterhouse and by hunters in the forest."

The question is sometimes raised that if the *ātmā* (soul) is completely transcendental to the material body, why should killing, if great pain is avoided, be considered wrongful violence? Even the *Bhagavad-gītā* states, "For the soul there is neither birth nor death. He is not slain when the body is slain." In his *Śrīmad-Bhāgavatam* purports, Śrīla Prabhupāda addresses this question: "All living entities have to fulfill a certain duration of being encaged in a particular type of material body. They have to finish the duration allotted in a particular body before being promoted or evolved to another body. Killing an animal or any other living being simply places an impediment in the way of his completing his term of imprisonment in a certain body. One should therefore not kill bodies for one's sense gratification, for this will implicate one in sinful activity." In short, killing an animal interrupts its progressive evolution through the species.

We can also appreciate the unjustness of animal killing by seeing that the body is a dwelling place for the soul. Individuals unexpectedly driven out of their comfortable homes suffer great inconvenience and distress. Such merciless and unjustified action is undoubtedly criminal. Furthermore, in order to receive their next material body, living beings must suffer extended prebirth tribulation. For the human being this involves months of being tightly packed in the darkness of the womb, where one is constantly disturbed by infections, acidic fluids burning the skin, jarring motions, and discomforts resulting from the mother's eating and drinking habits.

Is Killing Vegetables Wrong?

Another common metaphysical question is, "If all living entities are spiritually equal, then why is it acceptable to eat grains, vegetables, and fruits and not meat? Aren't vegetarians guilty of killing vegetables? In response, it may be pointed out that most vegetarian foods do not require killing. But even in those cases where a plant's life is taken, the pain involved is much less than when an animal is slaughtered, because the plant's nervous system is less developed. Clearly there is a vast difference between pulling a carrot out of the ground and killing a lamb. But still, one must undoubtedly suffer karmic reactions even for killing plants.

For this reason, Lord Kṛṣṇa explains in the *Bhagavad-gītā* that not only should humans eat only vegetarian foods, but they should offer these eatables to Him. If we follow this process of offering, the Supreme Lord, Kṛṣṇa, will protect us from whatever karmic reactions result from killing plants. Otherwise, according to the law of karma, we are personally responsible. The *Gītā* states, "The devotees of the Lord are released from all sins because they eat food that is offered first for sacrifice. Others, who prepare food for personal sense enjoyment, verily eat only sin."

Śrīla Prabhupāda elaborates on this principle of spiritual vegetarianism: "Human beings are provided with food grains, vegetables, fruits, and milk by the grace of the Lord, but it is the duty of human beings to acknowledge the mercy of the Lord. As a matter of gratitude, they should feel obliged to the Lord for their supply of foodstuff, and they must first offer Him food in sacrifice and then partake of the remnants." By eating such sanctified food – *prasāda* – one is protected from karmic reactions and one advances spiritually.

5

Beyond Vegetarianism

"If one offers Me with love and devotion a leaf, a flower, a fruit, or water, I will accept it."

— *Bhagavad-gītā* (9.26)

Beyond concerns of health, psychology, economics, ethics, and even karma, vegetarianism has a higher, spiritual dimension that can help us develop our natural appreciation and love for God. Walking through a supermarket, people may forget a very basic fact of nature – humankind doesn't make its own food, God does. There's something mystical about the way food grows. You put a tiny seed in the ground, it sprouts, and by the mysterious life force within it a food factory arises – a tomato plant producing dozens of tasty red tomatoes, an apple tree producing bushels of sweet apples. No team of scientists anywhere has yet invented anything as amazing as the simplest green creation of God.

But rather than admit the existence of a superior intelligence, scientists mislead the public with their theories of chemical evolution. Without substantial evidence, they proclaim that life comes from chemicals. Yet they cannot utilize those chemicals to make a seed that will grow into a stalk of wheat that will produce more seeds that will sprout into hundreds more stalks of wheat.

Once we admit that life comes only from life, it's entirely reasonable to suppose that all life originates from a common living source, the one Supreme Lord, known to the Muslims as Allah, to the Jews as Yahweh, to the Christians as Jehovah, and to the followers of the *Vedas* as Kṛṣṇa.

Out of gratitude we should at the very least offer our food to God. Every religion has a process of thanksgiving, but the spiritual path outlined in India's Vedic scriptures is unique in that the offering of food to the Lord is part of a highly developed form of yoga – one that helps us develop our personal loving relationship with God. This is called *bhakti-yoga*.

Originally, each soul has a direct relationship with God in the spiritual world, and according to the *Vedas*, the main purpose of life is to revive this lost relationship. The *Śrīmad-Bhāgavatam*, a classic Sanskrit work known as "the ripened fruit of the tree of Vedic knowledge," states, "The human form of life affords one a chance to return home, back to Godhead. Therefore every living entity, especially in the human form of life, must engage in devotional service."

Devotional service, or *bhakti-yoga*, is the highest form of yoga. In *Bhagavad-gītā*, after discussing various kinds of yoga, Lord Kṛṣṇa, the master of all yoga, declares, "And of all *yogīs*, the one with great faith who always abides in Me, thinks of Me within himself, and renders transcendental loving service to Me – he is the most intimately united with Me in yoga and is the highest of all." Lord Kṛṣṇa further states, "One can understand Me as I am, as the Supreme Personality of Godhead, only by devotional service. And when one is in full consciousness of Me by such devotion, he can enter into the kingdom of God."

The Yoga of Eating

Summarizing the process of *bhakti-yoga*, the Lord says, "All that you do, all that you eat, and all that you offer and give away, as well as all austerities that you may perform, should be done as an offering unto Me." So offering food is an integral part of the *bhakti-yoga* system.

The Lord also describes the types of offerings He will accept: "If one offers Me with love and devotion a leaf, a flower, a fruit, or water, I will accept it." Kṛṣṇa does not include meat, fish, or eggs in this list; therefore a devotee does not offer them to Him. Out of love, the devotee offers Kṛṣṇa only the purest and choicest foods – and these certainly do not include the weeks-old rotting corpses of slaughtered animals or the potential embryos of chickens.

In most religious systems people ask God to feed them ("Give us this day our daily bread"), but in Kṛṣṇa consciousness the devotee offers food to God as an expression of love for Him. Even in ordinary dealings, someone will prepare a meal for another as a sign of affection. It isn't only the meal itself that is appreciated, but the love and consideration that goes into it. In the same way, the process of offering food to God is intended to help us increase our love and devotion for Him. Of course, it is difficult to love someone we have never seen. Fortunately, the Vedic scriptures, unique in the world, describe God's personal features in great detail.

The Vedic conception of God is not vague. In the scriptures of other major religions God is described as the Supreme Father, but surprisingly little information is given about His personality. Christ spoke of himself as the son of God, and Muhammad referred to himself as Allah's prophet, and we know plenty about both of them. But what about God Himself? He appears only indirectly – as a voice from the heavens or a burning bush.

But despite this lack of information, God is a person with all the attributes of personhood, including a distinct form and appearance and all the powers and abilities His senses provide. If this is surprising, then ask yourself what kind of logical supposition it is that we the creatures have senses, form, and attributes, but our creator does not. Is it possible for the creature to surpass the creator? If we possess distinct forms and personalities, and God were not to possess them, we would be superior to Him in that respect. So just as we are persons, God is a person – the supreme person – with an infinitely powerful spiritual form. We have been created in His image.

Using their imaginations, Western artists have generally depicted God as a powerfully built old man with a beard. The Vedic scriptures provide another description. First, God is eternally youthful, and He possesses wonderful spiritual qualities that attract the minds of liberated souls. He is the supreme artist, the supreme musician, He speaks wonderfully and manifests unlimited intelligence, humor, and genius. Moreover, He displays incomparable transcendental pastimes with His eternal associates. There is no end to the descriptions of the attractive features of the Personality of Godhead found in the *Vedas*. Therefore He is called Kṛṣṇa, or "all-attractive." When we understand God's personal identity, it becomes much easier to meditate on Him, especially when offering Him food.

Because Kṛṣṇa is supremely powerful and completely spiritual, anything that comes in contact with Him also becomes completely pure and spiritual. Even in the realm of physical nature certain things have the ability to purify. For instance, the sun, with its powerful rays, can distill fresh, pure water from a lake contaminated with pollutants. If a material object like the sun can act in this way, then we can only imagine the purifying potency of the Supreme Personality of Godhead, who has effortlessly created millions of suns.

Spiritual Food

By His immense transcendental energies, Kṛṣṇa can actually convert matter into spirit. If we place an iron rod in fire, before long the iron rod becomes red hot and takes on all the essential qualities of fire. In the same way, the material substance we call food becomes completely spiritualized when offered to Kṛṣṇa. Such food is called *prasāda*, a Sanskrit word meaning "the mercy of the Lord."

Eating *prasāda* is a fundamental practice of *bhakti-yoga*. In other forms of yoga, one is required to restrain the senses, but *bhakti-yogīs* are free to use their senses in a variety of pleasing spiritual activities. For instance, they can use the tongue to taste delicious foods offered to Lord Kṛṣṇa. By such activities, the senses are gradually spiritualized and automatically attracted to divine pleasures that far surpass any material experience.

The Vedic scriptures contain many descriptions of *prasāda* and its effects. Lord Caitanya, an incarnation of the Supreme Lord who appeared in India five hundred years ago, said of *prasāda*, "Everyone has tasted these material substances before. However, in these ingredients there are extraordinary tastes and uncommon fragrances. Just taste them and see the difference in the experience. Apart from the taste, even the fragrance pleases the mind and makes one forget any other sweetness besides its own. Therefore it is to be understood that the spiritual nectar of Kṛṣṇa's lips has touched these ordinary ingredients and transferred to them all their spiritual qualities."

Eating only food offered to Kṛṣṇa is the ultimate perfection of a vegetarian diet. After all, even many animals such as pigeons and monkeys are vegetarian, so becoming a vegetarian is in itself not the greatest accomplishment. The *Vedas* inform us that the purpose of human life is reawakening the soul's original relationship with God, and only when we go beyond vegetarianism to *prasāda* can our eating be helpful in achieving this goal.

How to Prepare and Offer Prasāda

Our consciousness of the higher purpose of vegetarianism begins as we walk down the supermarket aisles selecting the foods we will offer to Kṛṣṇa. In the *Bhagavad-gītā* Lord Kṛṣṇa states that all foods can be classified according to the three modes of material nature – goodness, passion, and ignorance. Milk products, sugar, vegetables, fruits, nuts, and grains are foods in the mode of goodness and may be offered to Kṛṣṇa. As a general rule, foods in the modes of passion and ignorance are not offerable to Kṛṣṇa, who says in the *Gītā* that such eatables "cause pain, distress, and disease" and are "putrid, decomposed, and unclean." As may be guessed, meat, fish, and eggs are foods in the lower modes. But there are also a few vegetarian items that are classified in the lower modes – garlic and onions, for example. They should not be offered to Kṛṣṇa. (Asafetida, also called hing, is an acceptable substitute for onions and garlic and is available in most Oriental or Indian specialty shops.) Coffees and teas that contain caffeine are also considered to be in the lower modes. If you like hot beverages, purchase caffeine-free coffees and herbal teas.

In shopping, you should be aware that you may find meat, fish, and egg products mixed in with other foods, so be sure to study labels carefully. For instance, some brands of yogurt and sour cream contain gelatin, which is prepared from the horns, hooves, and bones of slaughtered animals. Make sure any cheese you purchase is rennetless, because rennet is an enzyme extracted from the stomach tissues of calves.

You should also avoid foods precooked by people who are not devotees of Kṛṣṇa. According to the subtle laws of nature, the cook acts upon the food not only physically but mentally. Food thus becomes an agency for subtle influences on our consciousness. To give another example of this principle, a painting is not simply a collection of strokes on a canvas; it is also an expression of the artist's state of mind. This mental content is absorbed by the person looking at the painting. Similarly, if we eat foods cooked by people devoid of spiritual consciousness – employees working in factories – then we are sure to absorb a dose of materialistic mental energies. As far as possible, use only fresh, natural ingredients.

In preparing food, cleanliness is the most important principle. Nothing impure should be offered to God, so keep your kitchen work area very clean. Always wash your hands thoroughly before preparing food. While preparing food, do not taste it. This is part of meditating that you are cooking the meal not for yourself but for Kṛṣṇa's pleasure. Kṛṣṇa should be the first to enjoy what you've cooked.

When the meal is prepared, you are ready to offer it. Arrange portions of the food on diningware kept especially for this purpose. (No one else should eat from these dishes.) The very simplest form of offering is to simply pray, "My dear Lord Kṛṣṇa, please accept this food." Remember that the real purpose of this is to show your devotion and gratitude to the Lord; the actual food you are offering is secondary. Without this devotional feeling, the offering will not be accepted. God is complete in Himself; He has no need of anything. Our offering is simply a means for us to show our love and gratitude toward Him. Following the offering one should chant for a few minutes the Hare Kṛṣṇa mantra: Hare Kṛṣṇa, Hare Kṛṣṇa, Kṛṣṇa Kṛṣṇa, Hare Hare/ Hare Rāma, Hare Rāma, Rāma Rāma, Hare Hare. Then the *prasāda* may be served. Try to appreciate the spiritual quality of *prasāda* by remembering how it frees one from the effects of karma. But above all, enjoy it.

Eventually you may wish to make a more formal offering according to the procedures established by the Hare Kṛṣṇa movement for persons who desire to practice Kṛṣṇa consciousness in their homes. Briefly, this involves setting up a simple altar with pictures of Lord Kṛṣṇa and the spiritual master, learning some simple Sanskrit mantras, and so forth. If you would like to learn how to do this, please contact the Kṛṣṇa temple nearest you or write to one of the addresses found in the front of this book.

Other Principles of Bhakti-yoga

Of course, offering *prasāda* is only part of the process of *bhakti-yoga.* In order to further purify your consciousness and spiritualize your senses, you can practice other items of devotional service. The first of these is the regular chanting of the Hare Kṛṣṇa mantra: Hare Kṛṣṇa, Hare Kṛṣṇa, Kṛṣṇa Kṛṣṇa, Hare Hare/ Hare Rāma, Hare Rāma, Rāma Rāma, Hare Hare. The *Kali-santaraṇa Upaniṣad* states, "These sixteen names composed of thirty-two syllables are the only means to counteract the evil effects of Kali-yuga [the present age of quarrel and hypocrisy]. In all the *Vedas* it is seen that to cross the ocean of nescience there is no alternative to the chanting of the holy name." The Hare Kṛṣṇa mantra may be chanted either congregationally, sometimes to the accompaniment of musical instruments, or quietly as a private meditation. For private meditation, the recommended procedure is to chant the Hare Kṛṣṇa mantra on beads especially made for this purpose. For further information, see the book by this publisher called *Chant and Be Happy,* which fully explains the process of Hare Kṛṣṇa mantra meditation.

To improve the quality of your spiritual life, you should also avoid the use of intoxicants – drugs, alcohol, and cigarettes, as well as soft drinks, coffee, and tea if they contain caffeine. Using these substances unnecessarily clouds the mind, which is already clouded with the material concept of life. The *Vedas* also recommend that a person attempting to advance in spiritual life have nothing to do with gambling, for it invariably puts one in anxiety and fuels greed, envy, and anger. Another activity that increases material desires and blocks the growth of spiritual awareness is illicit sex. The regulations of *bhakti-yoga* do, however, allow sex within marriage to bring children into the world.

By following the principles mentioned above, one can always experience increasing spiritual pleasure as a tangible part of one's life. In particular, one's offerings of food become more pleasing to Kṛṣṇa. God does not require the food we offer;

rather, He appreciates the degree of purity and devotion in our hearts as we offer it.

Eventually, one should take initiation from a bona fide spiritual master, without whose instruction and guidance it is not possible to attain the perfection of Kṛṣṇa consciousness. In the *Bhagavad-gītā* Lord Kṛṣṇa says, "Just try to learn the truth by approaching a spiritual master. Inquire from him submissively and render service unto him. The self-realized souls can impart knowledge unto you because they have seen the truth."

Śrīla Prabhupāda, renowned as India's greatest cultural and spiritual ambassador to the world, personally instructed his disciples in the art of preparing and distributing *prasāda*. Furthermore, in his books and public lectures, he extensively explained the Vedic philosophy underlying the practice of offering food to Kṛṣṇa. "We should remember then that it is not vegetarianism which is important," Śrīla Prabhupāda once said. "The important thing is that we simply have to try to learn how to love Kṛṣṇa. Love begins with give and take. We give something to our lover, he gives something to us, and in this way love develops." Anyone can enter into this loving transaction by offering vegetarian foods to Kṛṣṇa and accepting the remnants as *prasāda*.

6

A Higher Taste

Excerpts from the writings of His Divine Grace
A. C. Bhaktivedanta Swami Prabhupāda

The Myth of Scarcity

With the good will of the Supreme Personality of Godhead there can be enough fruits, grain, and other foodstuffs produced so that all the people in the world could not finish them, even if they ate ten times their capacity. In this material world there is actually no scarcity of anything but Kṛṣṇa consciousness. If people become Kṛṣṇa conscious, by the transcendental will of the Supreme Personality of Godhead there will be enough foodstuffs produced so that people will have no economic problems at all. One can very easily understand this fact. The production of fruits and flowers depends not upon our will but upon the supreme will of the Personality of Godhead. If He is pleased, He can supply enough fruits, flowers, etc., but if people are atheistic and godless, then nature, by His will, restricts the supply of food.

Caitanya-caritāmṛta (Ādi 9.38)

God Is Vegetarian

Mr. Faill: Is it necessary to follow certain eating habits to practice spiritual life?

Śrīla Prabhupāda: Yes, the whole process is meant to purify us, and eating is part of that purification. I think you have a saying, "You are what you eat," and that's a fact. Our bodily constitution and mental atmosphere are determined according to how and what we eat. Therefore the *śāstras* [scriptures] recommend that to become Kṛṣṇa conscious you should eat remnants of food left by Kṛṣṇa. If a tuberculosis patient eats something and you eat the remnants, you will be infected with tuberculosis. Similarly, if you eat food left by Kṛṣṇa [*kṛṣṇa-prasāda*], then you will be infected with Kṛṣṇa consciousness. Thus our process is that we don't eat anything immediately. First we offer the food to Kṛṣṇa, then we eat it. This helps us advance in Kṛṣṇa consciousness.

Mr. Faill: You are all vegetarians?

Śrīla Prabhupāda: Yes, because Kṛṣṇa is a vegetarian. Kṛṣṇa can eat anything because He is God, but in the *Bhagavad-gītā* [9.26] He says, "If one offers Me with love and devotion a leaf, a flower, a fruit, or water, I will accept it." He never says, "Give Me meat and wine."

The Science of Self-Realization (p. 159)

There Is no Scarcity

If we throw a bag of grain into the street, pigeons may come and eat four or five small grains and then go away. They will not take more than they can eat, and having eaten they go freely on their way. But if we were to put many bags of flour on the sidewalk and invite people to come and get them, one man would take ten or twenty bags and another would take fifteen or thirty bags and so on. But those who do not have the means to carry so much away will not be able to take more than a bag or two. Thus the distribution will be uneven. This is called advancement of civilization; we are even lacking in the knowledge which the pigeons, dogs, and cats have. Everything belongs to the Supreme Lord, and we can accept whatever we need, but not more. That is knowledge. By the Lord's arrangement the world is so made that there is no scarcity of anything. Everything is sufficient, provided that we know how to distribute it. However, the deplorable condition today is that one is taking more than he needs while another is starving.

Rāja-vidyā (p. 91)

"Thou Shalt Not Kill"

Śrīla Prabhupāda: We have to accept all the injunctions of the scripture as they are given, not only those that suit us. If you do not follow the first order, "Thou shalt not kill," then where is the question of love of God?

Visitor: Christians take this commandment to be applicable to human beings, not to animals.

Śrīla Prabhupāda: That would mean that Christ was not intelligent enough to use the right word: *murder*. There is *killing* and there is *murder*. *Murder* refers to human beings. Do you think Jesus was not intelligent enough to use the right word – *murder* – instead of the word *killing*? *Killing* means any kind of killing, and especially animal killing. If Jesus had meant simply the killing of humans, he would have used the word *murder*.... If you want to interpret these words, that is something else. We understand the direct meaning. "Thou shalt not kill" means "The Christians should not kill."

Father Emmanuel: Isn't the eating of plants also killing?

Śrīla Prabhupāda: The Vaiṣṇava philosophy teaches that we should not even kill plants unnecessarily. In the *Bhagavad-gītā* (9.26) Kṛṣṇa says: "If someone offers Me with love and devotion a leaf, a flower, a fruit, or a little water, I will accept it." We offer Kṛṣṇa only the kind of food He demands, and then we eat the remnants. If offering vegetarian food to Kṛṣṇa were sinful, then it would be Kṛṣṇa's sin, not ours. But God is *apāpa-viddha* – sinful reactions are not applicable to Him....Eating food first offered to the Lord is also something like a soldier's killing during wartime. In a war, when the commander orders a man to attack, the obedient soldier who kills the enemy will get a medal. But if the same soldier kills someone on his own, he will be punished. Similarly, when we eat only *prasāda* [the remnants of food offered to Kṛṣṇa], we do not commit any sin. This is confirmed in the *Bhagavad-gītā* (3.13): "The devotees of the Lord are released from all kinds of sins because they eat food that is first offered for sacrifice. Others, who prepare food for personal sense enjoyment, verily eat only sin."

Father Emmanuel: Kṛṣṇa cannot give permission to eat animals?

Śrīla Prabhupāda: Yes – in the animal kingdom. But the civilized human being, the religious human being, is not meant to kill and eat animals. If you stop killing animals and chant the holy name Christ, everything will be perfect.... I think the Christian priests should cooperate with the Kṛṣṇa consciousness movement. They should chant the name Christ or Christos and should stop condoning the slaughter of animals. This program follows the teachings of the Bible; it is not my philosophy. Please act accordingly and you will see how the world situation will change.

The Science of Self-Realization (pp. 111–15)

Physical Effects of Meat-Eating

Ample food grains can be produced through agricultural enterprises, and profuse supplies of milk, yogurt, and ghee can be arranged through cow protection. Abundant honey can be obtained if the forests are protected. Unfortunately, in modern civilization, men are busy killing the cows that are the source of yogurt, milk, and ghee, they are cutting down all the trees that supply honey, and they are opening factories to manufacture nuts, bolts, automobiles, and wine instead of engaging in agriculture. How can the people be happy? They must suffer from all the misery of materialism. Their bodies become wrinkled and gradually deteriorate until they become almost like dwarves, and a bad odor emanates from their bodies because of unclean perspiration resulting from eating all kinds of nasty things. This is not human civilization.

Śrīmad-Bhāgavatam (5.16.25)

Vegetarians Are Also Committing Violence

Sometimes the question is put before us: "You ask us not to eat meat, but you are eating vegetables. Do you think that is not violence?" The answer is that eating vegetables is violence, and vegetarians are also committing violence against other living entities because vegetables also have life. Nondevotees are killing cows, goats, and so many other animals for eating purposes, and a devotee, who is vegetarian, is also killing.... That is the law of nature. *Jīvo jīvasya jīvanam:* one living entity is the life for another living entity. But for a human being, that violence should be committed only as much as necessary.

Śrīmad-Bhāgavatam (3.29.15)

The Cow Should Be Protected

Milk is compared to nectar, which one can drink to become immortal. Of course, simply drinking milk will not make one immortal, but it can increase the duration of one's life. In modern civilization, men do not think milk to be important, and therefore they do not live very long. Although in this age men can live up to one hundred years, their duration of life is reduced because they do not drink large quantities of milk.... Instead of drinking milk, people prefer to slaughter an animal and eat its flesh. [*Editor's note: Beef has six times the cholesterol of milk. High cholesterol causes heart disease, America's major cause of death.*] The Supreme Personality of Godhead, in His instructions of *Bhagavad-gītā*, advises *go-rakṣya*, which means cow protection. The cow should be protected, milk should be drawn from the cows, and this milk should be prepared in various ways. One should take ample milk, and thus one can prolong one's life, develop his brain, execute devotional service, and ultimately attain the favor of the Supreme Personality of Godhead.

Śrīmad-Bhāgavatam (8.6.12)

Prasāda Frees One from Material Contamination

When there is an epidemic disease, an antiseptic vaccine protects a person from the attack of such an epidemic. Similarly, food offered to Lord Viṣṇu and then taken by us makes us sufficiently resistant to material infection, and one who is accustomed to this practice is called a devotee of the Lord. Therefore, a person in Kṛṣṇa consciousness, who eats only food offered to Kṛṣṇa, can counteract all reactions of past material infections, which are impediments to the progress of self-realization. On the other hand, one who does not do so continues to increase the volume of sinful action, and this prepares the next body to resemble hogs and dogs, to suffer the resultant reactions of all sins. The material world is full of contaminations, and one who is immunized by accepting *prasādam* of the Lord (food offered to Viṣṇu) is saved from the attack, whereas one who does not do so becomes subjected to contamination.

Bhagavad-gītā (3.14)

Those Who Kill Will Be Killed

If one kills many thousands of animals in a professional way so that other people can purchase the meat to eat, one must be ready to be killed in a similar way in his next life and in life after life. There are many rascals who violate their own religious principles. According to Judeo-Christian scriptures, it is clearly said, "Thou shalt not kill." Nonetheless, giving all kinds of excuses, even the heads of religions indulge in killing animals while trying to pass as saintly persons. This mockery and hypocrisy in human society bring about unlimited calamities; therefore occasionally there are great wars. Masses of such people go out onto battlefields and kill themselves. Presently they have discovered the atomic bomb, which is simply waiting to be used for wholesale destruction.

Caitanya-caritāmṛta (Madhya 24.251, purport)

Showing Devotion to God by Offering Food with Love

It is prescribed in *Bhagavad-gītā:* "If a devotee offers Me a small flower, a leaf, some water or a little fruit, I will accept it." The real purpose is to exhibit one's loving devotion to the Lord; the offerings themselves are secondary. If one has not developed loving devotion to the Lord and simply offers many kinds of foodstuffs, fruits, and flowers without real devotion, the offering will not be accepted by the Lord. We cannot bribe the Personality of Godhead. He is so great that our bribery has no value. Nor has He any scarcity; since He is full in Himself, what can we offer Him? Everything is produced by Him. We simply offer to show our love and gratitude to the Lord.

Śrīmad-Bhāgavatam (3.29.24)

Animal-Killing Is Not Civilized

Civilized men know the art of preparing nutritious foods from milk. For instance, on our New Vṛndāvana farm in West Virginia [*and on the other ISKCON farms throughout the world*], we make hundreds of first-class preparations from milk. Whenever visitors come, they are astonished that from milk such nice foods can be prepared. The blood of the cow is very nutritious, but civilized men utilize it in the form of milk. Milk is nothing but cow's blood transformed. You can make milk into so many things – yogurt, curd, ghee (clarified butter), and so on – and by combining these milk products with grains, fruits, and vegetables, you can make hundreds of preparations. This is civilized life – not directly killing an animal and eating its flesh.

The Science of Self-Realization (p. 12)

Offering Food to Kṛṣṇa Is an Exchange of Love

Kṛṣṇa is so kind that if anyone offers Him a leaf, a fruit, a flower, or some water, He will immediately accept it. The only condition is that these things should be offered with *bhakti* [devotion]. Otherwise, if one is puffed up with false prestige, thinking, "I have so much opulence, and I am giving something to Kṛṣṇa," one's offering will not be accepted by Kṛṣṇa....For anything offered to Kṛṣṇa with love and affection, Kṛṣṇa can reciprocate many millions of times over, both materially and spiritually. The basic principle involved is an exchange of love. Therefore Kṛṣṇa teaches in *Bhagavad-gītā* (9.27): "O son of Kuntī, all that you do, all that you eat, all that you offer and give away, as well as all austerities that you may perform, should be done as an offering unto Me."

Śrīmad-Bhāgavatam (10.11.11)

Animals Also Have the Right to Life

Interviewer: Another point in the Declaration of Independence is that all men are endowed by God with certain natural rights that cannot be taken away from them. These are the rights of life, liberty, and—

Śrīla Prabhupāda: But animals also have the right to life. Why don't animals also have the right to live? The rabbits, for instance, are living in their own way in the forest. Why does the government allow hunters to go and shoot them?

Interviewer: They were simply talking about human beings.

Śrīla Prabhupāda: Then they have no real philosophy. The narrow idea that my family or my brother is good, and that I can kill all others, is criminal. Suppose that for my family's sake I kill your father. Is that philosophy? Real philosophy is *suhṛdaṁ sarva-bhūtānām*: friendliness to all living entities.

The Science of Self-Realization (p. 180)

Satan's Philosophy

To be nonviolent to human beings and to be a killer or enemy of the poor animals is Satan's philosophy. In this age there is enmity toward poor animals, and therefore the poor creatures are always anxious. The reaction of the poor animals is being forced on human society, and therefore there is always the strain of cold or hot war between men, individually, collectively or nationally.

Śrīmad-Bhāgavatam (1.10.6)

Do Animals Have Souls?

Śrīla Prabhupāda: Some people say, "We believe that animals have no soul." That is not correct. They believe animals have no soul because they want to eat the animals, but actually animals do have a soul.

Reporter: How do you know that the animal has a soul?

Śrīla Prabhupāda: You can know, also. Here is the scientific proof ... The animal is eating, you are eating; the animal is sleeping, you are sleeping; the animal is defending, you are defending; the animal is having sex, you are having sex; the animals have children, you have children; they have a living place, you have a living place. If the animal's body is cut, there is blood; if your body is cut, there is blood. So, all these similarities are there. Now, why do you deny this one similarity, the presence of the soul? This is not logical. You have studied logic? In logic there is something called analogy. Analogy means drawing a conclusion by finding many points of similarity. If there are so many points of similarity between human beings and animals, why deny one similarity? That is not logic. That is not science.

The Science of Self-Realization (pp. 31)

The Danger of Starvation

In *Bhagavad-gītā* it is confirmed that one who takes foodstuff after a performance of sacrifice eats real food for proper maintenance of the body and soul, but one who cooks for himself and does not perform any sacrifice eats only lumps of sin in the shape of foodstuffs. Such sinful eating can never make one happy or free from scarcity. Famine is not due to an increase in population, as less intelligent economists think. When human society is grateful to the Lord for all His gifts for the maintenance of the living entities, then there is certainly no scarcity or want in society. But when men are unaware of the intrinsic value of such gifts from the Lord, surely they are in want. A person who has no God consciousness may live in opulence for the time being due to his past virtuous acts, but if one forgets his relationship with the Lord, certainly he must await the stage of starvation by the law of the powerful material nature.

Śrīmad-Bhāgavatam (3.5.49)

Killers of Animals are Stonehearted

Some rascals put forward the theory that an animal has no soul or is something like dead stone. In this way they rationalize that there is no sin in animal-killing. Actually animals are not dead stone, but the killers of animals are stonehearted. Consequently no reason or philosophy appeals to them. They continue keeping slaughterhouses and killing animals in the forest.

Śrīmad-Bhāgavatam (4.26.9)

The Animal-killer Will Become an Animal and Be Killed

By killing animals, not only will we be bereft of the human form but we will have to take an animal form and somehow or other be killed by the same type of animal we have killed. This is the law of nature. The Sanskrit word *māmsa* means "meat." It is said, *mām sah khadati iti māmsah*. That is, "I am now eating the flesh of an animal who will some day in the future be eating my flesh."

Caitanya-caritāmṛta (Madhya 24.252)

There Is Already Enough Food

As human society is presently structured, there is sufficient production of grains all over the world. Therefore the opening of slaughterhouses cannot be supported. In some nations there is so much surplus grain that sometimes extra grain is thrown into the sea, and sometimes the government forbids further production of grain. The conclusion is that the earth produces sufficient grain to feed the entire population, but the distribution of this grain is restricted due to trade regulations and a desire for profit. Consequently in some places there is scarcity of grain and in others profuse production. If there were one government on the surface of the earth to handle the distribution of grain, there would be no question of scarcity, no necessity to open slaughterhouses, and no need to present false theories about overpopulation.

Śrīmad-Bhāgavatam (4.17.25)

A Diet to Cure the Disease of the Soul

Everyone should know that there are two kinds of diseases in human society. One disease, which is called *adhyātmika*, or material disease, pertains to the body, but the main disease is spiritual. The living entity is eternal, but somehow or other, when in contact with the material energy, he is subjected to the repetition of birth, death, old age and disease.... The Kṛṣṇa consciousness movement has taken up the mission of curing this disease, but people are not very appreciative because they do not know what this disease is. A diseased person needs both proper medicine and a proper diet, and therefore the Kṛṣṇa consciousness movement supplies materially stricken people with the medicine of the chanting of the holy name, or the Hare Kṛṣṇa *mahā-mantra*, and the diet of *prasādam*.

Caitanya-caritāmṛta (Ādi 10.51)

Elevation to the Transcendental Position

Our Kṛṣṇa consciousness movement acts on this principle. We simply give people the chance to hear about the Supreme Personality of Godhead and give them *prasādam* to eat, and the actual result is that all over the world people are responding to this process and becoming pure devotees of Lord Kṛṣṇa. We have opened hundreds of centers all over the world just to give people in general a chance to hear about Kṛṣṇa and accept Kṛṣṇa's *prasādam*. These two processes can be accepted by anyone, even a child. It doesn't matter whether one is poor or rich, learned or foolish, black or white, old or still a child – anyone who simply hears about the Supreme Personality of Godhead and takes *prasādam* is certainly elevated to the transcendental position of devotional service.

Caitanya-caritāmṛta (Ādi 7.141)

Spiritual Food

A flower accepted for one's sense gratification is material, but when the same flower is offered to the Supreme Personality of Godhead by a devotee, it is spiritual. Food taken and cooked for oneself is material, but food cooked for the Supreme Lord is spiritual *prasāda*. This is a question of realization.

Śrīmad-Bhāgavatam (8.12.8)

An Ideal Diet

The purpose of food is to increase the duration of life, purify the mind, and aid bodily strength. This is its only purpose. In the past, great authorities selected those foods that best aid health and increase life's duration, such as milk products, sugar, rice, wheat, fruits, and vegetables.

…Animal fat is available in the form of milk, which is the most wonderful of all foods. Milk, butter, cheese, and similar products give animal fat in a form which rules out any need for the killing of innocent creatures.…Protein is amply available through split peas, dāl, whole wheat, etc.

…The best food is the remnants of what is offered to the Supreme Personality of Godhead. In *Bhagavad-gītā* the Supreme Lord says that He accepts preparations of vegetables, flour, and milk when offered with devotion.…Of course, devotion and love are the chief things which the Supreme Personality of

Godhead accepts....Therefore to make food antiseptic, eatable, and palatable for all persons, one should offer food to the Supreme Personality of Godhead.

Bhagavad-gītā (17.10)

Food Offered to Kṛṣṇa Becomes Transcendental

In the *Bhagavad-gītā* (9.26) Kṛṣṇa says: "If one offers Me with love and devotion a leaf, a flower, a fruit, or water, I will accept it." (Bg. 9.26) The Lord is *pūrṇa*, complete, and therefore He eats everything offered by His devotees. However, by the touch of His transcendental hand, all the food remains exactly as before. It is the quality that is changed. Before the food was offered, it was something else, but after it is offered the food acquires a transcendental quality. Because the Lord is *pūrṇa*, He remains the same even after eating....The food offered to Kṛṣṇa is qualitatively as good as Kṛṣṇa; just as Kṛṣṇa is indestructible, the food eaten by Kṛṣṇa, being identical with Him, remains as before.

Apart from this, Kṛṣṇa can eat the food with any one of His transcendental senses. He can eat by seeing the food or by touching it. Nor should one think that it is necessary for Kṛṣṇa to eat. He does not become hungry like an ordinary human being; nonetheless, He presents Himself as being hungry, and as such, He can eat everything and anything, regardless of quantity.

Caitanya-caritāmṛta (Madhya 4.77)

7

Recipes

Notes on Ingredients

While many of the ingredients listed in the recipes will be familiar to you and easily available at food stores, some may be new. Therefore we have included a glossary of such ingredients, along with information about where to purchase them, at the end of the recipe section.

Specially Prepared Ingredients

In some recipes in *The Higher Taste* curd cheese and ghee are two easy-to-make basic ingredients for which there are no substitutes. Curd cheese is a natural, light, protein-rich cheese, and ghee is the purified essence of butter. The butter you bring home from the store is 80 percent butterfat, 18 percent water, and 2 percent protein solids. If you cook the butter slowly, the water it contains will boil off and the protein solids separate from the butterfat – and you will be left with a fragrant golden liquid that is the preferred cooking medium for many of the dishes in this book. Most commonly used in Indian cuisine, ghee is also popular in Middle Eastern cooking. While olive, sesame, peanut, and coconut oils have all found their way into the recipes in this book, because of ghee's delightful, slightly nutty flavor, it is the perfect medium in which to cook traditional Indian sweets and savories. While ghee can be purchased at most gourmet, Indian, and Middle Eastern grocers – and even at some well-stocked supermarkets – it's easy to make at home (and much more economical). Unsalted butter makes the best ghee. Ghee does not require refrigeration (it will keep for six months unrefrigerated and up to a year if frozen), so don't be shy to make a large batch. No cooking oil can match ghee for its pleasant taste and ease of digestion.

Making ghee

½–2 kg (1–5 pounds) unsalted butter

Cut the butter into large chunks and melt it over moderate heat in a large, heavy-bottomed saucepan, stirring to ensure that it melts slowly and does not brown. Still stirring, bring the melted butter to a boil. When the butter becomes frothy, reduce the heat to very low. Simmer uncovered and undisturbed for the required time until the solids have settled on the bottom, a thin crust appears on the top, and the ghee is clear and golden.

Skim the surface crust with a fine-mesh wire sieve and set it aside in a bowl.

Turn off the heat and remove the ghee with a ladle without disturbing the solids on the bottom. Pour the ghee through a sieve lined with paper towels. When you have removed all the ghee that you can without disturbing the solids, allow the ghee to cool and store it in a suitable covered storage container.

The remaining ghee and solids can be mixed with the top crust and used for vegetables or soups, or as a sandwich spread. This portion of the ghee will keep for 3–4 days in the refrigerator.

Making Homemade Curd Cheese (Panir)

You need little by way of equipment to make curd cheese: a 2–6 liter/quart pan or larger (depending on the quantity of milk), a stirring paddle or wooden spoon, a colander, and several folds of new cheesecloth. You will need the following ingredients for an easily manageable home batch of panir.

> 4 liters/quarts fresh milk
> 3–4 cups yogurt or 4–6 tablespoons lemon juice
>   or 2 teaspoons citric acid dissolved in ⅓ cup water

Pour the milk into a heavy-bottomed pan that allows plenty of room for boiling. Set it over high heat and bring the milk to a full foaming boil, stirring often to prevent scorching and sticking. Reduce the heat to low, and before the foam subsides, drizzle in the lemon juice or citric acid solution, or spoon in the yogurt.

Very gently and slowly move the spoon through the milk in one direction. After 10 or 15 seconds, remove the pan from the heat and continue to gently agitate the milk until large lumps of soft curd form. If the cheese has not formed after 1 minute, place the pan over the heat again momentarily until the casein (milk protein) coagulates and leaves a pale yellow-green whey. If necessary, add a little more acid agent.

Remove the pan from the heat as soon as the cheese forms. Cover it and set it aside for 10 minutes. If you want a very soft cheese, gently pour in 1 or 2 cups of hot water. When the cheese has settled under the surface of the whey, it is ready to drain.

Line a colander with 2 or 3 thicknesses of cheesecloth or some clean white cloth that has been dipped in water and wrung dry. Drape the corners and edges of the cloth over the sides of the colander. If you want to collect the whey, set the colander over another pan; otherwise place it in a sink. (Many sweet-makers in Bengal use the whey to make further batches of cheese, but you need a significant amount more whey than lemon juice to do the job – you need one part whey to four parts milk.)

Remove the large lumps of cheese with a slotted spoon and place them in the colander. Gently pour the smaller pieces and remaining whey into the colander.

Add any fresh herbs now, and fold in well.

Gather up the corners of the cloth and twist it around. Hold the bag of cheese under a gentle stream of cold running water for 5 to 10 seconds. Gently twist the cloth to squeeze out the excess whey.

Drain the cheese slowly, allowing it to compact under its own weight by hanging the bag over a bowl to drain. Otherwise, for a quicker result, you can place the bag of cheese under a weight until firm (about 20 minutes).

Unwrap the cheese and use as directed, or wrap in paper-towel-lined plastic wrap, Ziploc bags, or plastic containers and refrigerate for up to 4 days.

Asian Lunch

Hot and Sour Tom Yum Soup

Stir-fried Hokkien Noodles with Asian Greens and Tofu

Salad of Vietnamese Greens

Curry Puffs with Quick Tamarind Chutney

Thai Sticky Rice with Mango

Hot and Sour Tom Yum Soup

In Thai cuisine, most soups are served as a side dish as part of a full meal. They are meant to be light and refreshing to counterbalance heavier, richer dishes. This vegetarian version of the well-known tom yum is full of bold, strong flavors – coriander roots, lemon grass, chili, kaffir lime leaves, and sorrel. Serves 6.

> 4 scraped coriander roots
> 4 sticks lemon grass, white parts only
> 1 teaspoon yellow asafetida powder
> 2 or 3 small, fresh, hot red chilies, chopped
> 2 liters/quarts rich vegetable stock (recipe follows)
> 4 kaffir lime leaves
> 4 large ripe tomatoes, blanched, peeled, and coarsely chopped
> 400 g (13 ounces) firm pressed tofu, cut
>   into 2.5 cm (1-inch) pieces
> 1 bunch sorrel, torn
> 2 or 3 small, fresh, hot red chilies, sliced diagonally
> 5 tablespoons soy sauce
> ½ cup lime juice
> ⅔ cup chopped fresh coriander (cilantro) leaves

Pound the coriander roots, lemon grass, asafetida, and chilies to make a rough paste using a mortar and pestle, or process in a blender with a few drops of water.

Boil the vegetable stock in a saucepan over full heat. Drop in the kaffir lime leaves and tomato and cook for 2 or 3 minutes.

Add the spice paste, reduce the heat to a simmer, add the tofu and sorrel, and cook for another 2 minutes.

To serve: Divide the extra chilies, soy sauce, lime juice, and chopped coriander into large, deep serving bowls, and pour the boiling soup over. Serve with hot steamed rice.

Vegetable Stock
This is a basic Vietnamese vegetable stock known as *nuoc leo rau cai.*

> *4 liters/ quarts water*
> *1 cup carrots, sliced*
> *1 cup cabbage, sliced*
> *½ cup celery stalk, sliced*
> *¼ cup white radish, sliced*
> *1½ teaspoons salt*

Combine all the ingredients in a saucepan and boil for 1 hour or until the liquid is reduced by half. Strain and set aside.

Stir-fried Hokkien Noodles with Asian Greens and Tofu

Plump, yellow *hokkien* noodles have been described as "the spaghetti of the noodle world" – they're thick and succulent, with a substantial "meatiness" to them. Serves 4.

> *500 g (1 pound) eggless Hokkien noodles*
> *2 tablespoons Chinese black beans, coarsely*
> *   chopped (do not rinse)*
> *¼ cup white grape juice or water*
> *½ teaspoon yellow asafetida powder*
> *1 tablespoon finely chopped fresh ginger*
> *1 teaspoon fresh red chili, seeded and finely chopped*
> *¾ cup rich vegetable stock*
> *2 tablespoons soy sauce*
> *1 teaspoon sugar*
> *1 teaspoon Chinese sesame oil*
> *2½ tablespoons peanut oil*
> *500 g (1 pound) choy sum, or Chinese greens of*
> *   your choice, trimmed*
> *500 g (1 pound) firm fresh tofu, cubed 2 cm (¾-inch)*

Place the noodles in a heatproof bowl, cover with boiling water, and let stand for 1 minute. Drain.

Soak the chopped black beans in the grape juice or water for 10 minutes, then strain and reserve the separated beans and liquid.

Mix together the drained beans, asafetida powder, ginger, and fresh chili.

Combine the vegetable stock, soy sauce, sugar, sesame oil, and reserved black-bean soaking liquid.

Heat a large wok or frying pan until very hot, add 1 tablespoon peanut oil, and just before it starts to smoke, add the dry black bean mixture and stir over medium heat for 30 seconds or until fragrant.

Add the choy sum, drained noodles, and liquid stock mixture, stir briefly, cover, and simmer for 2 minutes or until the greens are just wilted. Remove the lid, add the tofu, stir carefully, and simmer for a further 2–3 minutes, uncovered, until the sauce is slightly reduced and the noodles are tender. If you want a less juicy dish, stir in a mixture of one tablespoon each of cornflour (cornstarch) and water.

Serve: Place the noodles in warm serving bowls and serve immediately.

Salad of Vietnamese Greens

The wonderful thing about this salad is its simplicity. Serves 4.

200 g (7 ounces) bean sprouts
1 packed cup basil leaves
¾ packed cup Vietnamese mint leaves*
¾ packed cup coriander (cilantro) leaves

2 fresh, small red chilies, sliced
1 lime, quartered

Wash and thoroughly drain all the vegetables and herbs. Combine all the ingredients. Serve on 4 individual platters with a wedge of lime each.

---

* Vietnamese mint is also known as *rau ram* (pronounced *row-ram*) and *laksa* leaf.

Curry Puffs with Quick Tamarind Chutney

Our recipe testers polished off these Malaysian delicacies in record time. If you're looking for a finger food par excellence, look no further. Makes about 40 bite-size puffs.

1 cup sweet potato, diced very small
1 cup carrot, diced very small
1 cup potato, diced very small
1 cup peas
1 tablespoon oil
fresh curry leaves from 3 large sprigs, torn
1 tablespoon grated fresh ginger
½ teaspoon yellow asafetida powder
2 tablespoons Malaysian hot curry powder
2 teaspoons sugar
1 teaspoon salt
5 sheets ready-made puff pastry
ghee or oil for deep-frying
Quick Tamarind Chutney, to serve (recipe follows)

The filling

Steam the vegetables separately until tender. Drain.

Heat the oil in a frying pan over moderate heat. When the oil is hot, drop in the curry leaves and fry until they crackle, sprinkle in the ginger, fry for 1 minute or until aromatic, then add the yellow asafetida powder and fry momentarily.

Stir in the curry powder, all the cooked vegetables, and the sugar and salt. Fry together for 1 or 2 minutes, then remove from heat. Allow mixture to cool.

The puffs
Cut the sheets of puff pastry into 8-cm (3-inch) squares.

Place 2 teaspoons of cooled filling in the center of each square. Fold diagonally into triangles and seal, pressing the edge with fork tines, or seal to make semicircles with a decorative pinched and fluted edge.

Heat the oil for deep-frying in a wok or deep-frying pan over moderate heat until fairly hot. Fry the puffs in batches for 2–3 minutes or until puffed and golden brown. Remove and drain on paper towels.

Serve hot, warm, or cold with the accompanying tamarind chutney or a sweet chili sauce.

For a less traditional but lower-fat version, try baking your curry puffs in a moderate oven.

Quick Tamarind Chutney
Simultaneously hot, sweet, sour, and spicy. Makes 1 cup.

¼ cup dried tamarind, soaked in 2 cups boiling water for ½ hour
½ teaspoon ground cumin
2 teaspoons ginger juice (juice squeezed from
    about 2 tablespoons shredded ginger)
3 tablespoons brown sugar
½ teaspoon salt
big pinch chili powder

Pour the soaked tamarind through a sieve, collecting the juice. Rub and squeeze the remaining pulp to extract the tamarind purée. Discard the pulp.

Combine the tamarind purée with the remaining ingredients in a medium saucepan. Cook over moderately high heat for 10–15 minutes or until reduced by half. Serve at room temperature.

Thai Sticky Rice with Mango

This simple and sublime dessert is popular, in one form or another, all over Southeast Asia. Glutinous rice is available at Asian grocers, and is eaten not just as dessert but as a sweet afternoon snack or at any time. Serves 4.

> 2 cups sticky (glutinous) white rice, soaked
>   in cold water for 1 hour, then drained
> 1¼ cups coconut milk (one 400 ml can)
> pinch salt
> 2 tablespoons sugar
> 2 large ripe mangoes
> 2 tablespoons coconut milk to serve
> mint leaves to decorate

Combine rice, coconut milk, salt, and sugar in an uncovered saucepan with 1¼ cups of water. Stir and bring to a boil over moderate heat.

Simmer the rice, stirring, for about 8–10 minutes or until all the liquid has been absorbed. Remove from heat, cover pan, and let stand for 5 minutes.

Transfer the rice to a steamer or double saucepan (boiler). Steam for 15–20 minutes.

Spoon the hot, steamed, sticky rice into 6–8 individual ramekins or pudding molds lined with plastic wrap and set aside to cool.

Serve: Remove rice from mold, and place one portion in the center of each dessert plate. Arrange the mango around it. Drizzle rice with reserved coconut milk. Garnish with mint leaves.

Alternatively, press the warm rice evenly into a tray lined with plastic wrap. When cold, cut into diamonds.

Indian Dinner

Jaipur-style Quick and Easy Mung Dāl

Rice with Green Peas and Almonds

North Indian Curried Cauliflower and Potatoes

Creamed Spinach with Curd Cheese (Palak Panir)

Griddle-Baked Bread (Chapati)

Hot and Sweet Pineapple Chutney

Walnut and Raisin Semolina Halava

Jaipur-style Quick and Easy Mung Dāl

Jaipur is the famed Pink City in Rajasthan, India. In its enormous City Palace – literally a small city within a city – is the present home of the Maharaj of Jaipur. In the center of the compound, surrounded by gardens, sits the spectacular Sri Radha-Govinda Temple. I fondly remember my visits to Jaipur, its stunning architecture, dedicated residents, and its delicious vegetarian cuisine. Serves 6.

> 1 cup split mung beans, soaked in water
>   for 1 hour, rinsed and drained
> 7 cups water
> ½ teaspoon turmeric powder
> 1 cup carrots, diced
> 2 cups small cauliflower florets
> 1 tablespoon ghee or oil
> 2 tablespoons cumin seeds
> ½ teaspoon fennel seeds
> 1 or 2 green chilies, seeded and chopped
> 1 tablespoon chopped fresh ginger
> ¼ cup chopped fresh coriander leaves
> 2 tablespoons fresh lemon juice
> 1 teaspoon salt
> ¼ teaspoon black pepper

Combine the mung dāl, water, turmeric, and carrots in a heavy, medium-sized saucepan and bring to a boil. Reduce the heat and simmer, half-covered, for 15 minutes or until the dāl starts to break down.

Add the cauliflower and cook 10 more minutes.

Season as follows: Heat the ghee or oil in a small saucepan over moderate heat. Sprinkle in the cumin and fennel seeds, and fry them until they darken a few shades. Add the chilies and ginger and fry until aromatic.

Pour the contents of the whole saucepan into the simmering soup. Add the fresh coriander (cilantro) leaves, lemon juice, salt, and pepper.

Serve hot in warmed soup bowls, with rice or bread.

Rice with Green Peas and Almonds

Lightly spiced basmati rice studded with green peas and almonds never fails to receive praise. It's ideal for catering or for a special lunch or dinner. Serves 4–5.

> 1 cup basmati or other long-grain white rice
> ¾ teaspoon salt
> 4 green cardamom pods, slightly crushed
> 2 cups water
> ¼ teaspoon turmeric
> 2 teaspoons ghee or oil
> one 4 cm (1½-inch) cinnamon stick
> 6 whole cloves
> ⅓ cup slivered or sliced raw almonds
> 1 cup fresh or frozen peas

Bring to a boil the water, salt, and turmeric in a 2-liter/quart saucepan over moderate heat. Keep pan covered to avoid evaporation.

Heat ghee or oil in another 2-liter/quart saucepan over moderately low heat. Fry cinnamon stick, cloves, cardamom pods, and almonds in hot ghee until almonds turn a pale golden-brown. Add rice and sauté for about 2 minutes or until the grains turn translucent.

Pour in boiling water, and if using fresh peas, add them now. Stir, increase heat to high, and bring the water to a full boil. Immediately reduce the heat to low, cover with a tight-fitting lid, and gently simmer, without stirring, for 15–20 minutes or until all the water is absorbed and the rice is tender and flaky. If using frozen peas, quickly sprinkle them over the rice halfway through the cooking time. Turn off the heat, allow the rice to steam for another 5 minutes.

Serve hot.

North Indian Curried Cauliflower and Potatoes

This is a popular North Indian vegetable dish that goes well with hot flatbreads (chapatis), a light *dāl*, and a salad. Serve it any time of day for any occasion. Serves 4–5.

> 1 tablespoon ghee or oil
> ½ teaspoon black mustard seeds
> 1 teaspoon cumin seeds
> 1 teaspoon minced fresh ginger
> 2 hot green chilies, seeded and chopped
> 3 medium potatoes, diced
> 1 medium cauliflower, cut into small florets
> 2 medium tomatoes blanched, peeled, and diced
> ½ teaspoon turmeric
> ½ teaspoon garam masala
> 2 teaspoons ground coriander
> 1 teaspoon brown sugar
> 2 teaspoons salt
> 2 tablespoons coarsely chopped fresh coriander or parsley
> 1 tablespoon fresh lemon juice

Heat ghee or oil in a large, heavy saucepan over moderate heat. When ghee is hot, add mustard seeds. When they crackle, add cumin and sauté until cumin seeds darken a few shades. Add ginger and chilies, sauté for a few moments, then add potato and cauliflower pieces.

Stir-fry the vegetables for 4–5 minutes or until vegetables start to stick to bottom of pan.

Add tomatoes, turmeric, garam masala, ground coriander, sugar, and salt. Mix well, reduce heat to low, cover saucepan, and stirring occasionally, cook for 10–15 minutes or until vegetables are tender. Add water if necessary during cooking, but don't over-stir vegetables. When vegetables are cooked, add the fresh coriander and lemon juice.

Serve hot.

Creamed Spinach with Curd Cheese (Palak Panir)

Spinach with homemade curd cheese and cream is one of North India's favorite vegetable dishes. There are dozens of regional varieties. Here's a simple, quick-cooking version. Serve with rice or hot flat-breads. Serves 5–6.

> 1 teaspoon chopped fresh ginger
> 1 fresh hot green chili, seeded and minced
> 1 teaspoon ground coriander
> ½ teaspoon sweet paprika
> ½ teaspoon ground cumin
> ½ teaspoon turmeric
> 2 teaspoons ghee or oil
> 2 large bunches of spinach, washed, trimmed, and chopped
> 4 tablespoons cream
> fresh homemade curd cheese (panir) made from 2 liters
>   (8 cups) milk, cut into 1.25-cm (½-inch) cubes (see
>   method, p. 69)
> ½ teaspoon garam masala
> 1 teaspoon salt

Steam spinach in a saucepan with a little water for 4–5 minutes or until soft and reduced in size.

Blend spinach in a food processor or blender until smooth. Remove and set aside. Clean the food processor.

Blend ginger and chili in food processor or blender and process with a few teaspoons of cold water. Add the coriander, paprika, cumin, and turmeric and blend to form a smooth paste. Scrape the paste into a bowl.

Heat ghee in a large saucepan over moderate heat. When ghee is hot, add spice paste and fry for 2–3 minutes or until paste is aromatic and starts to stick. Fold in puréed spinach, combining it with the spices. Cook over full heat for 3–4 minutes.

Fold in cream, panir cubes, garam masala, and salt. Cook for an additional 5 minutes and serve hot.

Griddle-Baked Bread (Chapati)

Chapatis are one of India's most popular breads, enjoyed especially in the northern and central regions. They are partially cooked on a hot griddle and finished over an open-heat source. Chapatis are made from a special wholemeal (whole-wheat) flour called *atta*, available from Indian grocers. If unavailable, substitute sifted wholemeal flour. Makes 12 chapatis.

> 2 cups sifted chapati flour (atta) or wholemeal flour
> ½ teaspoon salt (optional)
> water
> extra flour for dusting
> melted butter or ghee (optional, for spreading
>   over chapatis after cooking)

Combine flour and salt in a mixing bowl. Add up to ⅔ cup water, slowly pouring in just enough to form a soft, kneadable dough. Turn the dough onto a clean working surface.

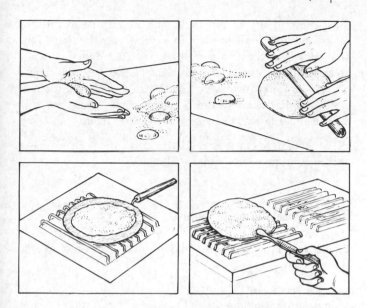

Knead the dough for about 8 minutes or until silky-smooth. Cover with an overturned bowl and leave for ½–3 hours.

Re-knead dough for 1 minute. Divide dough into 12 portions. Roll each portion into a smooth ball and cover with a damp cloth.

Preheat a griddle or nonstick heavy frying pan over moderately low heat for 3–4 minutes. Flatten a ball of dough, dredge it with flour, and carefully roll it out into a thin, perfectly even, smooth disk about 15 cm (6 inches) in diameter.

Carefully pick up the chapati and slap it between your hands to remove the excess flour. Slip it onto the hot plate, avoiding wrinkling it. Cook for about 1 minute on the first side. The top of the chapati should start to show small bubbles. Turn the chapati over with tongs. Cook it until small brown spots appear on the underside (about 1 minute).

Turn a second burner onto high, pick up the chapati with the tongs, and hold it about 5 cm (2 inches) over the flame. The chapati will swell into a puffy balloon. Continue to cook the chapati until it is speckled with black flecks. Place the cooked chapati in a bowl or basket, cover with a clean tea towel or cloth, and then cook the rest of the chapatis. When they're all cooked and stacked, you might like to butter them.

Serve chapatis hot for best results, or cover and keep warm in a preheated warm oven for up to ½ hour.

Hot and Sweet Pineapple Chutney

Pineapple chutney should be "too hot to bear, but too sweet to resist." Makes 2 cups.

>   2 teaspoons ghee or oil
>   2 teaspoons cumin seeds
>   4 broken dried red chilies or as desired
>   1 large ripe pineapple, peeled, cored, and cubed
>   ½ teaspoon ground cinnamon
>   ½ teaspoon ground cloves
>   ⅔ cup brown sugar
>   ⅓ cup raisins

Heat ghee in a 2-liter/quart heavy-based saucepan over moderate heat until hot but not smoking. Fry cumin seeds in hot ghee until they darken slightly. Add chilies and cook until golden brown. Add pineapple pieces, ground cinnamon, and cloves.

Gently boil the chutney, stirring occasionally, over moderate heat for about 45 minutes, or until the pineapple becomes soft and the juice evaporates. Stir constantly as the chutney dries and the pineapple starts to stick to the bottom.

Add the sugar and raisins and cook for another 10–15 minutes, or until the chutney is thick and jamlike. Remove from the heat and allow the chutney to cool.

Serve at room temperature.

Walnut and Raisin Semolina Halava

Semolina halava is one of the most popular desserts served at Hare Krishna restaurants worldwide. This version of the famous hot, fluffy pudding with juicy raisins, raw sugar, and walnut pieces rates high in the "halava top ten."

The secret of good halava is to roast the semolina very slowly for at least 20 minutes, with enough butter so as not to scorch the grains. Steam the finished halava over very low heat with a tight-fitting lid for 5 minutes to fully plump the semolina grains; then allow it to sit covered for another 5 minutes. Fluffy, plump-grained halava is best served hot, with a spoonful of cream or custard. Serves 6–8.

> 2¾ cups water
> 1¼ cups raw (Turbinado) sugar
> ½ cup raisins
> 140 g (7 tablespoons) unsalted butter
> 1¼ cups coarse-grained semolina
> ⅓ cup walnut pieces

Combine water, sugar, and raisins in a 2-liter/quart saucepan. Place over moderate heat, stirring to dissolve the sugar.

Bring to a boil, then cover with a tight-fitting lid and remove from heat.

Melt the butter in a 2- or 3-liter/quart nonstick saucepan over fairly low heat without scorching it. Add the semolina.

Slowly and rhythmically stir-fry the grains until they darken to a tan color and become aromatic (about 20 minutes). Add walnut pieces about halfway through roasting. Stirring more carefully, raise the heat under the grains.

Turn on the heat under the sugar water and bring to a rolling boil. Remove saucepan of semolina and butter from heat, slowly pouring the hot syrup into the semolina, stirring steadily. The grains may splutter at first, but will quickly stop as the liquid is absorbed.

Return pan to stove and stir steadily over low heat until the grains fully absorb the liquid, start to form a puddinglike consistency, and pull away from the sides of the pan.

Place a tight-fitting lid on the saucepan and cook over the lowest possible heat for 5 minutes. Turn off heat and allow the halava to steam, covered, for an additional 5 minutes.

Serve hot in dessert bowls as it is or with the toppings suggested above.

Middle Eastern Banquet

Turkish Pilaf with Currants and Pine Nuts

Lebanese Eggplant Dip (Babagannouj)

Chickpea and Sesame Paste (Hummus bi Tahini)

Couscous with Vegetable Sauce

Israeli Chickpea Croquettes (Falafel)

Lebanese Bulgur-Wheat Salad (Tabbouleh)

Fruit Compote with Fragrant Syrian Milk Pudding

Turkish Pilaf with Currants and Pine Nuts

Pine nuts can be toasted lightly in a dry frying pan or with a little olive oil to release a deeper, nuttier flavor. Coupled with flavorful cloves, orange, ginger, thyme, and succulent currants, they add a tasty crunch to this exotic rice dish from Turkey. Serves 6.

> 3 cups vegetable stock or water
> 1 tablespoon extra virgin olive oil
> ½ cup pine nuts
> ½ teaspoon yellow asafetida powder
> 1½ cups basmati rice or other good-quality
>   long-grain white rice
> 4 whole cloves
> one 2.5-cm (1-inch) cube ginger, sliced
> 2 bay leaves
> 2 whole 10-cm (4-inch) stalks fresh thyme
> three 3-inch strips orange zest
> 1½ teaspoons salt
> ½ teaspoon freshly-ground black pepper
> ⅓ cup currants
> 3 tablespoons chopped continental (flat-leaf) parsley

Bring to a boil the vegetable stock in a small saucepan over moderate heat. Cover and reduce to a simmer.

Heat half the olive oil in a 2-liter/quart saucepan over low to moderate heat. When slightly hot, add the pine nuts. Toast them in the oil for 1–2 minutes or until light golden-brown and fragrant. Remove saucepan from heat, quickly remove nuts from oil with a slotted spoon, and drain them on paper towels. Return pan and remaining oil to heat.

Warm remaining oil and sprinkle asafetida into the hot oil. Stir momentarily, drop in the rice, and stir for 2–3 minutes, or until the rice grains turn translucent.

Pour the boiling stock into the rice. Add cloves, ginger, bay leaves, thyme stalks, orange zest, salt, and pepper. Raise heat to high and quickly bring rice to a full boil. Immediately reduce heat to very low and cover pan with a tight-fitting lid.

Gently simmer rice, without stirring, for 20–25 minutes or until liquid is fully absorbed and rice is tender and fluffy.

Remove saucepan from heat, allowing the delicate rice grains to firm up for 5 minutes. Lift the lid and carefully extract the cloves, thyme stalks, ginger, and bay leaves, which should be sitting on top.

Carefully fold in currants, nuts, and continental parsley, and serve hot.

Lebanese Eggplant Dip (Babagannouj)

This version of the famous Middle Eastern *mezze* (hors d'oeuvre) can be served as an appetizer with breads, salads, and a variety of other nourishing and substantial dishes. It has a characteristic smoky flavor from roasting the eggplants until they blacken. Serves 4.

> 2 large eggplants (*aubergines*)
> a little olive oil
> ½ cup tahini
> juice of 2 large lemons
> ½ teaspoon salt
> ¼ teaspoon coarsely ground black pepper
> ½ teaspoon yellow asafetida powder
> 1 tablespoon finely chopped fresh parsley
> 1 teaspoon paprika or cayenne pepper

Slit eggplants with a sharp knife to allow the steam to escape while baking.

Lightly oil eggplants, then place them in a preheated oven at 200°C/390°F.

Bake for 40 minutes or until the outsides are charred and crisp.

Remove eggplants from oven, scoop pulp into a bowl (it should have a smoky aroma), and mash thoroughly.

Mix eggplant pulp with the tahini, lemon juice, salt, pepper, asafetida, and parsley until smooth. If the mixture is too thick, add a little water. Spoon the dip into a serving bowl, pour the olive oil into the center, and garnish with paprika or cayenne.

Serve immediately.

Chickpea & Sesame Paste (Hummus bi Tahini)

Chickpeas are a great source of protein, iron, fiber, vitamins A and B_6, riboflavin, thiamin, niacin, calcium, phosphorus, sodium, and potassium. One cup of chickpeas has the useable protein equivalent of one 30 g (4 -ounce) steak. When combined with dairy products, their usable protein increases. This famous spread works well as a dip or spread on bread or crackers. Makes about 1 cups.

> 200 g dried chickpeas (1 very heaped metric measuring cup)
> ¼ cup lemon juice
> ½ teaspoon yellow asafetida powder
> 6 tablespoons tahini
> 1 teaspoon salt

Soak chickpeas in cold water overnight or for at least 12 hours.

Drain and place chickpeas in a large saucepan. Cover with cold water, about three times the volume of chickpeas, and bring to a boil. Reduce to a simmer and cook for an hour or until the chickpeas are tender, topping up with water whenever necessary.

Drain chickpeas, reserving cooking liquid. Cool slightly, then rub the chickpeas to loosen their skins. Cover with cold water. The loose skins will rise to the surface. Scoop them off and discard.

Place peeled chickpeas in a food processor with the lemon juice, asafetida, tahini, and half the salt. Process to a smooth purée, adding some of the reserved cooking liquid if necessary to achieve a smooth result. Add the remaining salt later if needed.

Couscous with Vegetable Sauce

Whereas rice is eaten in many Arab countries, couscous is the preferred grain of North African cuisine. Couscous is made from semolina, and it is also the name of the famous dish of which couscous is the main ingredient. Imported couscous can be purchased in most supermarkets. Here, it's cooked using the "quick" method.

Couscous is always served in a mound with sauce poured on top, and the extra juice from the vegetables is sometimes served separately in small bowls on the side. Serve couscous as a filling main course with a spoonful of the ubiquitous North African hot pepper sauce, harissa. Serves 8–10.

Sauce
1 tablespoon butter or oil
½ teaspoon yellow asafetida powder
6 small zucchinis, sliced
2 medium green peppers, seeded, cored, and cut into thick strips
2 cups pumpkin, cubed

1 large potato, peeled and coarsely chopped
2 small turnips, cut in half and sliced lengthwise
at least 4 cups water
2 cups chickpeas, cooked and drained
8 medium tomatoes, diced
1½ teaspoons ground coriander
1½ teaspoons ground cumin
2 teaspoons turmeric
½ teaspoon cayenne pepper
2 small hot green chilies, chopped
1½ teaspoons salt
½ teaspoon freshly ground black pepper

Couscous

2 cups water
1 teaspoon oil
1 teaspoon salt
2 cups couscous
1–2 tablespoons extra butter or oil (optional)

Prepare the sauce

Heat butter or oil over moderate heat in a heavy saucepan. Add the asafetida, zucchinis, peppers, pumpkin, potato, and turnips, and sauté for 10 minutes. Add half the water and bring to a boil. Reduce the heat and simmer for 30 minutes.

Add chickpeas, tomatoes, ground coriander, cumin, turmeric, cayenne, chilies, salt, pepper, and the rest of the water (adding more if needed). Stir well, and reduce the heat to a simmer. Cook for another 15 minutes. Toward the end of the sauce's cooking time, prepare the couscous.

Prepare the couscous

Heat 2 cups water in a large saucepan. Add oil and salt and bring to a boil. Remove from heat.

Carefully whisk in the couscous. Cover tightly with a lid and set aside for 2 minutes to allow the grains to swell. Remove the lid and add 2–3 tablespoons butter. Heat the grains over low heat for 3 minutes, stirring with a fork.

Assemble the dish

Pile the couscous on a large, pre-warmed serving dish. Drain some of the liquid from the vegetables (reserving it in small bowls to serve as an accompaniment), and pour the vegetable sauce over the couscous. Serve immediately.

Israeli Chickpea Croquettes (Falafel)

These spicy chickpea croquettes are delicious served stuffed inside split Middle Eastern flatbreads, dressed with tahini sauce or hummus, and accompanied by a green salad. Do not use canned or cooked chickpeas for this recipe. Makes 14–16 falafel.

> 1¼ cups raw chickpeas, soaked overnight and drained
> ½ teaspoon yellow asafetida powder
> ¾ cup finely chopped parsley
> 1 teaspoon ground coriander
> 1 teaspoon ground cumin
> ¼ teaspoon cayenne pepper
> 1½ teaspoons salt
> ¼ teaspoon freshly ground black pepper
> ½ teaspoon baking powder
> oil for deep-frying

Process chickpeas in a food processor and mince finely. Scrape minced chickpeas into a bowl. Fold in the herbs, spices, salt, and baking powder. Mix well, knead, and leave for 30 minutes.

Form the mixture into 14–16 falafel balls. If they're too sticky, roll the balls in a little flour. Repeat until all the mixture is rolled.

Heat a heavy pan or wok with oil to a depth of 6.5–7.5 cm (2½–3 inches), until moderately hot 180°C/355°F. Deep-fry 6–8 falafels at a time, turning when required, for 5–6 minutes or until evenly golden brown.

Remove and drain on paper towels. Cook all the falafel. Serve hot, as recommended above.

Lebanese Bulgur-Wheat Salad (Tabbouleh)

This Lebanese salad is probably the most famous of all Middle Eastern *mezze* (hors d'oeuvres). Bulgur wheat (parched, ground, parboiled wheat grains) is not only tasty and substantial but nutritious – rich in protein, calcium, phosphorus, iron, potassium, niacin, and vitamins B_1 and B_2. Bulgur-wheat salad is easy to prepare and is characterized by its fresh lemon-mint-parsley flavor. Tabbouleh is traditionally served on fresh, crisp lettuce leaves. Add more lemon juice if necessary to assure the authentic fresh-lemon taste. Serves 6.

> 1¼ cups fine bulgur wheat
> ½ teaspoon yellow asafetida powder
> ¼–½ cup fresh lemon juice
> ¼ cup olive oil
> 1½ teaspoons salt
> ¼ teaspoon coarsely ground black pepper
> 3 cups finely chopped parsley
> 3 tablespoons fresh mint
> 2 teaspoons sumac (optional)
> 1 cup seeded, unpeeled cucumber, diced
>   into 1.25-cm (½-inch) cubes
> 2 medium tomatoes, diced
> lettuce leaves for decoration

Soak the bulgur wheat for 1½ hours in warm water. Drain and squeeze out moisture. Dry it further by spreading it on a cloth and patting it dry.

Combine the soaked wheat, asafetida, lemon juice, olive oil, salt, pepper, parsley, mint, and sumac in a large bowl and mix well. Add the cucumber and tomatoes and toss. Chill and serve with lettuce leaves.

Fruit Compote with Fragrant Syrian Milk Pudding

Succulent stewed dried fruits couple wonderfully with Middle Eastern rice flour pudding known as *muhallabeya*. Every community has its own traditional flavorings and presentation for this pudding, some flavoring it with orange-blossom water, others rose water, and some sprinkling it with chopped almonds or pistachios. The Turkish version uses vanilla or lemon zest, whereas the Iranians prefer cardamom. Serves 6.

> 1¼ cups dried figs
> 1 cup sugar
> 1 vanilla bean, split
> 1 cinnamon stick
> fine zest from 1 orange and half a lemon
> juice from 1 orange and half a lemon
> ½ cup pitted prunes
> ½ cup dried apricots
> ¾ cup dried peaches

Soak figs in hot water for 1 hour. Drain.

Combine sugar, vanilla bean, cinnamon stick, zest, and citrus juice in a saucepan, along with 1½ cups of water.

Bring to a boil, then reduce the heat and simmer for 10 minutes. Add the figs along with the dried fruits, and simmer with a tightly fitting lid for ½ hour or until the fruits are tender. Cool to room temperature.

Serve with the fragrant milk pudding (recipe follows).

Fragrant Syrian Milk Pudding (Muhallabeya)
    scant 1¼ cups rice flour
    4¾ cups cold milk
    ½ cup sugar
    1–2 tablespoons pure distilled rosewater
    1–2 tablespoons chopped pistachio nuts

Whisk the rice flour with a cup of the cold milk, adding it gradually and mixing thoroughly to avoid lumps.

Bring to a boil the rest of the milk in your heaviest pan.

Whisk in the rice flour and milk mixture, stirring vigorously. Cook on very low heat, stirring constantly for 10–15 minutes or until mixture thickens. Whisk in the sugar until dissolved, then remove saucepan from heat and pour in rosewater.

Whisk the whole mixture until creamy smooth, and chill.

To serve: transfer the pudding to a large serving bowl or individual bowls and sprinkle with the chopped pistachios. Serve as an accompaniment to the fruit compote.

European Winter Banquet

Old-fashioned Cream of Pumpkin Soup

Vegetables au Gratin

Herbed Bread Rolls

Italian Market Salad

Carob Fudge Cake

Spiced Hot Apple Juice Drink

Old-fashioned Cream of Pumpkin Soup

Pumpkin soup is a great winter favorite. Milk and a simple seasoning of black pepper and nutmeg allow the pumpkin flavor to predominate. Serves 4.

> 3 cups water
> 1½ cups milk
> 2 tablespoons butter
> ¼ teaspoon nutmeg
> ¼ teaspoon freshly ground black pepper
> 4 cups (1 kg or 2.2 pounds) pumpkin, peeled,
>   seeded, and cubed
> 1 tablespoon plain (white) flour
> 1 teaspoon salt
> 1 tablespoon light cream
> 2 tablespoons chopped fresh parsley

Melt half the butter in a 6-liter/quart saucepan over moderate heat. Add the nutmeg, black pepper, and pumpkin cubes and sauté for 10 minutes. Add the water and bring to a boil, cooking until the pumpkin is very tender.

Empty contents of saucepan into a blender and add half the milk. Purée the mixture carefully. Remove and set aside. Rinse the saucepan.

Heat remaining butter in the saucepan over moderate heat. Stir flour into butter. Return pumpkin purée to saucepan along with remaining milk, stirring constantly until the soup is well blended. Bring to a boil, simmer for a few minutes, and season with salt.

Serve the hot soup in individual, prewarmed soup bowls, garnished with light cream and chopped parsley.

Vegetables au Gratin

· ·

This rich favorite consists of lightly steamed vegetables in a Mornay sauce, topped with grated cheese and baked until golden brown. It combines wonderfully with a light soup and bread accompaniment. Serves 6–8.

> 8 cups assorted vegetables cut into large, bite-sized chunks
> (try a selection from the following: cauliflower, broccoli,
> carrots, French [string] beans, green peas, baby potatoes,
> asparagus, squash, pumpkin, sweet potato)
> ⅓–⅔ cup butter
> ¼ teaspoon yellow asafetida powder
> ¼ teaspoon nutmeg
> ⅔ cup plain (white) flour
> 5 cups (1.25 liters) warm milk
> 2 teaspoons salt
> ¾ teaspoon ground white pepper
> 250 g (9 ounces) grated cheddar cheese
> 1 tablespoon extra butter (optional)
> 2 tablespoons chopped fresh parsley

Lightly steam the vegetables until cooked but still a little firm.

Melt butter in a medium saucepan over moderate heat. Remove pan from heat. Add the asafetida powder and nutmeg. Stir in the flour with a wooden spoon to make a smooth paste. Gradually add the milk, stirring constantly.

Return the pan to the heat and bring the sauce to a boil, still stirring. Reduce the heat to low and simmer, stirring constantly, for 1 minute or until the sauce is thick and smooth. Add the salt, pepper, and half the grated cheese. Add the steamed vegetables and mix well.

Spoon the vegetables into a buttered baking dish. Cover them with the remaining grated cheese and dot with little pieces of butter.

Bake in a preheated, hot oven 205°C/400°F for 25 minutes or until the top is golden brown.

Garnish with chopped fresh parsley and serve hot.

Herbed Bread Rolls

In this recipe, small, bun-sized pieces of herbed and yeasted dough are arranged in a quiche pan or shallow cake pan and baked. They come to the table joined together in a singular circular cluster, and diners can each break off their own roll. Makes 18 rolls.

> 1 teaspoon dried yeast
> about 1¼ cups warm water
> 1 teaspoon sugar
> 3 cups unbleached plain (white) bread flour
> 1 teaspoon salt
> 3 teaspoons oil
> 1 teaspoon fresh thyme leaves, minced
> 1 teaspoon fresh oregano leaves, minced
> 2 teaspoons fresh basil leaves, chopped
> ½ teaspoon yellow asafetida powder
> poppy seeds, sesame seeds, fine oatmeal,
>   or dried herbs for topping

Combine yeast, a few teaspoons of warm water, and the sugar in a small bowl. Set aside for 10 minutes, or until the mixture is frothy.

Whisk together flour and salt.

Add oil, herbs, and asafetida to the frothy yeast mixture.

Lord Kṛṣṇa

Lord Kṛṣṇa explains to His friend Arjuna
in the *Bhagavad-gītā* (9.26), "If one offers
Me with love and devotion a leaf, a flower,
a fruit, or water, I will accept it."

Right: Israeli Chickpea Croquettes (p. 95)

Below: Stuffed Italian Flatbread (Focaccia) (p. 141)

Bottom: Mozzarella and Tomato Pizza (p. 147)

Top: Herbed Bread Rolls (p. 102)

Above: Griddle-baked bread
(Chapati) (p. 84)

Left: Crispy Curd-Cheese Fritters
(Panir Pakoras) (p. 133)

Above left: Salad of Vietnamese Greens (p. 74)

Above: Turkish Pilaf with Currants and Pine Nuts (p. 90)

Left: Mexican Green Chili Rice (Arroz Verde) (p. 108)

Below: Gauranga Potatoes (p. 132)

Above: Malaysian Sweet, Sour, and Hot Salad (Rojak) (p. 126)

Right: Mung Beans, Rice, and Vegetables (Khichari) (p. 134)

Below left: Greek-style White Bean and Vegetable Soup (p. 116)

Below right: Hot and Sour Tom Yum Soup (p. 72)

Above: Rich and Tasty Lasagna with Grilled Vegetables (p. 143)

Right: Curry Puffs with Quick Tamarind Chutney (p. 75)

Below: Vegetables au Gratin (p. 101)

Above: Carob Fudge Cake (p. 105)

Left: Thai Sticky Rice with Mango (p. 77)

Below left: Fruit Compote with Fragrant Syrian Milk Pudding (p. 97)

Below right: Walnut and Raisin Semolina Halava (p. 87)

Left: Classic Rose Lassi (p. 151)

Below left: Moist and Luscious Maple Fruit Muffins (p. 130)

Below right: Quick Cherry Cheesecake (p. 149)

Make a well in the center of the flour and pour in the yeast mixture. Add three-quarters of the warm water and mix. Add enough of the remaining water, if required, to make a soft but nonsticky dough. Knead the dough for 5 minutes or until smooth.

Place the dough in an oiled bowl, cover with plastic wrap, and leave in a warm place for one hour or until doubled in size.

Punch down the dough and divide into 18 even-sized pieces. Shape them by rolling them around under cupped hands on a floured board or marble slab, then arrange them fairly close together in a lightly oiled, 25-cm (10-inch) quiche pan or round, shallow baking dish. Keep in mind that the rolls will approximately double in size.

Allow the rolls to rise again for about 30 minutes. Spray with water and sprinkle with poppy seeds, sesame, fine oatmeal, or dried herbs.

Preheat the oven to 220° C/430° F and bake the rolls for 30–35 minutes or until golden brown and hollow-sounding when tapped on the underside. Serve.

Italian Market Salad

This delicious combination of fresh greens, steamed vegetables, and feta cheese marinated in a delicious lemon-and-oil dressing should be served with crusty bread rolls. Makes enough for 6 persons.

1 medium zucchini, cut into long wedges
2 medium carrots, peeled and cut into long wedges
2 stalks celery, cut into thin slices diagonally
½ cup snow peas (mange toutes), tips and strings removed
1 cup artichoke hearts marinated
    in brine, drained, and quartered

1 cup of cubed feta cheese
3 radishes, sliced
2 or 3 inner lettuce leaves, sliced into paper-thin strips
2 medium green chilies, seeded and
    sliced into long paper-thin strips
½ cup cherry tomatoes, halved
¼ cup olive oil
½ teaspoon yellow asafetida powder
¼ cup fresh lemon juice
1 tablespoon chopped fresh basil
1 teaspoon dry mustard,
    mixed with 2 teaspoons cold water
1 teaspoon salt
½ teaspoon freshly ground black pepper
crisp lettuce leaves for serving
fresh basil leaves for garnish
½ cup pitted black olives for garnish

Lightly blanch carrots and celery in a large pan of boiling, lightly salted water until the vegetables are crisp but tender (about 2 minutes). During the last minute, add the zucchini wedges and snow peas (mange toutes). Remove pan from heat and drain the vegetables. Refresh under cold water and drain again. Allow the vegetables to cool thoroughly.

Combine artichoke hearts, feta cheese, radishes, sliced lettuce, green chilies, tomatoes, and steamed vegetables in a large bowl.

Blend the olive oil, asafetida, lemon juice, basil, mustard paste, salt, and pepper in a bowl.

Toss the vegetables and the dressing. Cover and marinate in the refrigerator for at least one hour.

Serve on individual lettuce leaves garnished with fresh whole basil leaves and black olives.

Carob Fudge Cake

··

This two-tiered carob cake is light in texture without the use of eggs. The cake's light texture is due to the sour milk. Filled and iced with Carob Vienna Icing, it is an irresistible dessert. Makes one two-tiered 20-cm (8-inch) carob fudge cake.

> *125 g (6–7 tablespoons) butter, room temperature*
> *1 cup caster (superfine) sugar*
> *1 teaspoon vanilla essence*
> *1 cup carob powder*
> *½ cup hot water*
> *2 teaspoons fresh lemon juice*
> *1 cup milk*
> *1⅔ cups plain (white) flour*
> *1 teaspoon baking powder*
> *1 teaspoon bicarbonate of soda (baking soda)*
> *pinch salt*
> *jam and cream for filling*
> *Carob Vienna Icing (recipe follows)*

Preheat oven to 180°C/355°F.

Cream butter, sugar, and vanilla until light and fluffy.

Whisk carob powder into the hot water and mix to a smooth paste.

Fold together carob mixture and butter-sugar mixture.

Combine the lemon juice with the milk to sour it (this makes an excellent egg replacer).

Sift the flour, baking powder, bicarbonate of soda (baking soda), and salt, and add it to the creamed mixture alternately with the sour milk. Mix thoroughly.

Spoon the cake mixture into two buttered 20-cm (8-inch) cake tins.

Bake for 30 minutes or until the tops spring back when lightly pressed. Allow the cakes to cool in their tins for 10 minutes.

Turn out and allow to cool completely. Fill with jam and cream and ice with Carob Vienna Icing.

Carob Vienna Icing
  125 g (6 tablespoons) butter
  2½ cups icing (confectioner's) sugar
  4 tablespoons carob powder
  2 tablespoons hot water

Beat the butter until creamy. Sift the sugar. Blend the carob powder with the hot water. Add the icing sugar to the butter alternately with the carob mixture until it reaches a spreading consistency.

Spiced Hot Apple Juice Drink

Use freshly squeezed or bottled apple juice for this winter's-night beverage. Serves 6.

  6 cups apple juice
  one 10 cm (4-inch) cinnamon stick
  6 whole cloves
  ¼ teaspoon whole cardamom seeds
  lemon slices
  honey as sweetener, if required

Bring to a boil apple juice and spices in a large, heavy-based saucepan over high heat. Cover the pan and reduce the heat to low, simmering for 20 minutes.

Just before serving, strain the spices from the juice. Serve hot with slices of lemon and the optional honey.

Latin American Buffet

Mexican Green Chili Rice (Arroz Verde)

Sweet Potato Soup with Corn and Chilies

Cheddar and Jalapeño Chili Biscuits

Cheesy Bean and Tortilla Stacks (Tostadas)

Chilled Papaya Refresher (Refresco de Papaya)

Mexican Green Chili Rice (Arroz Verde)

....

Arroz verde (literally "green rice") is colored with spinach, fresh parsley, and coriander leaves, and flavored with fresh, very mild, large green chilies, such as poblano or Anaheim. If these chili varieties are unavailable, use any large, mild green chilies you can find. Serves: 4–6.

> *3 large mild fresh green chilies*
> *3 or 4 large spinach leaves, thoroughly washed and drained*
> *1 cup chopped parsley*
> *½ cup chopped fresh coriander leaves*
> *3 cups vegetable broth or stock*
> *1½ teaspoons salt*
> *2 teaspoons olive oil*
> *½ teaspoon yellow asafetida powder*
> *1½ cups long-grain white rice*
> *¼ teaspoon coarsely ground black pepper*

Roast the chilies over a burning gas jet on your stove, holding them with a pair of kitchen tongs (or place them under the grill [broiler]), until they brown a little. Transfer them to a plastic bag and seal the bag. When the chilies are cool, remove them from the bag and peel them, remove the seeds, and cut them into thin strips. Put aside in a small bowl.

Process spinach leaves and half the herbs in a food processor with a little of the vegetable stock to make a purée.

Transfer this green purée along with the remaining stock and the salt to a 2-liter/quart saucepan over moderate heat and bring to a boil.

Heat the oil in another 2-liter/quart saucepan over moderate heat. When hot, sprinkle in the asafetida, stir momentarily, then add the rice and fry for 2–3 minutes, or until translucent.

Pour in the boiling vegetable stock. Increase the heat to full, bring to a boil, cover with a lid, and reduce the heat to a gentle simmer.

Cook the rice without stirring for 15–20 minutes or until the grains are soft, dry, and tender.

Remove the pan from the heat and set aside for 5 minutes. Remove the lid, stir in the remaining herbs and black pepper.

Serve hot, garnishing each serving with strips of roasted chilies.

Sweet Potato Soup with Corn and Chilies

The sweet potato, like the ordinary potato, was cultivated in prehistoric Peru but is now grown around the world in hundreds of varieties. The most common are yellow and white. Generally, the paler the flesh, the drier the flesh. The darker tubers become moister and sweeter when cooked.

Sweet potatoes combine beautifully with another South American favorite – fresh corn. For contrasting texture, I have left the corn kernels whole in this tasty soup, but if you prefer, you can blend the corn to a purée with the sweet potatoes. Serves 4–6.

1 tablespoon butter or oil
1 teaspoon yellow asafetida powder
4–5 cups sweet potato, diced
4 cups rich vegetable stock
1¼ cups cooked corn kernels
1 green jalapeño chili, seeded and finely diced
1½ teaspoons salt (less if using a salty stock)
½ teaspoon freshly ground black pepper
whole coriander leaves for garnish

Heat the butter in a 3-liter/quart saucepan over moderate heat.

Sprinkle in the asafetida and drop in the sweet potatoes. Fry the potatoes for 2–3 minutes, then add the vegetable stock. Bring to a boil and cook for 15–20 minutes, or until the sweet potatoes are tender but not broken down. Remove the saucepan from the heat. Strain the sweet potatoes, being careful to reserve all the liquid. Return the cooking liquid to the rinsed-out saucepan.

Process the sweet potatoes along with some of the cooking liquid in a food processor and reduce to a purée.

Add the sweet potato purée to the cooking liquid and return to moderate heat. Add the cooked corn, chili, salt, and pepper.

Simmer the soup for another 10 minutes.

Serve hot with crusty bread and a garnish of fresh coriander leaves.

Cheddar and Jalapeño Chili Biscuits

I was dubious when I was sent this recipe for chili biscuits by a little old lady from Pasadena, but she assured me that they were delicious. After cooking my first batch I had to agree. Makes about 18 biscuits.

> 1 cup plain (white) flour
> ½ cup yellow cornmeal (polenta)
> 2 teaspoons baking powder
> ½ teaspoon baking soda
> ½ teaspoon salt
> 2 tablespoons cold unsalted butter, cut into bits
> 1½ cups grated extra tasty cheddar cheese
> 2 or 3 pickled 4 cm (1½-inch) jalapeño chilies, minced
> 2 or 3 fresh 4 cm (1½-inch) jalapeño chilies, minced
> ⅔ cup milk

Preheat oven to 220°C/425°F.

Sift together flour, cornmeal, baking powder, baking soda, and salt in a bowl. Rub in the butter and combine thoroughly until the mixture resembles coarse meal.

Stir in the cheese and chilies, add the milk, and stir until the mixture forms a soft, sticky dough.

Drop the dough by rounded tablespoons onto a buttered baking sheet.

Bake in the center of the oven for 15–20 minutes or until pale golden.

Serve at room temperature.

Cheesy Bean and Tortilla Stacks (Tostadas)

A popular Mexican combination – a stack of "refried" beans (*frijoles refritos*) – crispy lettuce, guacamole, sour cream, spicy sauce, and cheese piled onto a crispy fried corn tortilla. Don't even dream of not making a mess – serve with plenty of napkins! Makes 6 tostadas.

> 6 large corn tortillas
> oil for pan-frying
> frijoles refritos (recipe follows)
> 4 medium tomatoes, chopped or cut into thin wedges
> 2 cups shredded iceberg lettuce
> 2 ripe, medium avocados, mashed with a little salt, pepper, and lemon, or guacamole (recipe follows)
> ¼–½ cup light sour cream
> spicy tomato sauce (recipe follows)
> 1 cup grated tasty cheddar cheese

Heat sufficient oil in a frying pan to pan-fry the tortillas. When the oil is hot, drop in a tortilla.

Fry it until golden brown on both sides. Remove from the oil with tongs, shake off excess oil, and while still hot, press into a bowl to produce a shallow cup shape. Remove when firm. Repeat for all the tortillas.

Stack the tortillas as follows: a layer of *frijoles refritos*, some tomato pieces, shredded lettuce, a spoon of avocado or guacamole next to a dollop of sour cream, a large spoonful of tomato sauce, and a generous pile of grated cheese.

Serve immediately.

Guacamole
   2 ripe medium avocados, peeled, stoned, and mashed
   2 tablespoons finely shredded iceberg lettuce leaves
   1 or 2 small green chilies, seeded and finely chopped
   2 teaspoons fresh lemon or lime juice
   ¼ teaspoon yellow asafetida powder
   ½ teaspoon salt
   ¼ teaspoon freshly ground black pepper

Combine all the ingredients.

"Refried" Beans (frijoles refritos)
   2 teaspoons butter or oil
   ¼ teaspoon yellow asafetida powder
   2 cups cooked pinto or red kidney beans
   1 teaspoon chili powder or less to taste
   ½ teaspoon cumin powder
   ½ teaspoon salt

Heat butter or oil in a frying pan over moderately high heat. Sprinkle in the asafetida, stir in half the beans, a few tablespoons of water, the chili powder, cumin, and salt.

Fry the beans until they start to stick to the pan, and then partially mash them with a masher.

Add the rest of the beans and a little more water. Continue frying, scraping the pan to prevent sticking and incorporating all the beans. When the beans are a thick chunky paste, remove from the heat.

Spicy Tomato Sauce
    1 teaspoon olive oil
    1 teaspoon green chili, seeded and minced
    ¼ teaspoon yellow asafetida powder
    1 teaspoon chili powder, or less to taste
    1 cup tomato purée
    ½ teaspoon lemon juice
    ½ teaspoon salt
    1 teaspoon sugar

Heat the oil in a small saucepan over moderate heat. Sprinkle in the green chili, fry for 30 seconds, sprinkle in the asafetida, chili powder, and tomato purée, and bring to a boil. Reduce to a simmer.

Cook the sauce uncovered for 5 minutes or until somewhat reduced. Add the lemon juice, salt, and sugar and remove from the heat.

Chilled Papaya Refresher (Refresco de Papaya)

Ripe papayas, whether red, orange, or yellow, are beautifully sweet. When choosing papayas, select fruits that are soft enough to hold an impression from gentle thumb or finger pressure. Their aroma should be pronounced and musky sweet. This refreshing drink from Guatemala is flavored with lime and pure vanilla. If limes are unavailable, replace with lemons. Serve icy cold. *Refresco!* Serves 4–6.

> 1 large ripe papaya, about 700 g (1½ pounds)
> ⅔ cup very cold buttermilk or skim milk
> ½ cup sugar
> black pulp scraped from 1 plump vanilla
>   bean, or 1 teaspoon vanilla sugar
> 2 cups crushed ice
> 5 tablespoons strained fresh lime juice
> ½ teaspoon finely grated lime zest
> thin slices of lime for garnish (optional)

Peel the papaya, cut in half, remove the seeds, and chop coarsely.

In a blender set on high, process the fruit with the buttermilk or skim milk, sugar, vanilla, and ice until the fruit is smooth. Add the lime juice and zest and process again until smooth and thick.

Pour into tall, chilled glasses and serve at once, garnished with lime slices if desired.

Greek Dinner

Greek-style White Bean and Vegetable Soup (Fasoulada)

served with Crusty Bread, Cheese, and Kalamata Olives

Warm Vegetable Salad with Greek-style Oil and Lemon Dressing

Greek-style Eggplant Casserole (Moussaka)

Nut Pastries in Syrup (Baklava)

Greek-style White Bean and Vegetable Soup (Fasoulada)

Probably every Greek housewife has a version of *fasoulada*, a full-bodied, thick rustic soup of white beans and vegetables. Any white beans are suitable, such as cannellini, black-eyed beans, lima, navy, or haricot. You can serve *fasoulada* as an entrée, or you can build a substantial meal around it by adding bread, olives, and cheese. Serves 6.

> 2 cups haricot or white beans of your choice,
>   soaked overnight
> ½ teaspoon yellow asafetida powder
> 1½ cups chopped, peeled tomatoes
> ¾ cup diced carrot
> 1 cup chopped celery, including leaves
> 2 tablespoons tomato paste
> ¼ cup chopped parsley
> 1–2 tablespoons virgin olive oil
> ¼ teaspoon freshly ground black pepper
> ½ teaspoon sugar
> 1½ teaspoons salt
> chopped parsley for garnish

Drain and rinse the soaked beans. Place them in a 5-liter/quart saucepan along with about 8 cups of water, and bring to a boil over full heat.

Add all the other ingredients to the pan except the salt and garnish. Return the pan to full heat, bring to a boil, then reduce the heat to a simmer and cook, tightly covered, for about 1 hour or until the beans are soft.

Stir in the salt, and sprinkle each bowl of hot soup with some of the reserved parsley.

Warm Vegetable Salad with Greek-style Oil and Lemon Dressing

Greek oregano, *rigani*, is a stronger, sharper version of the Italian herb. The word oregano derives from the Greek, meaning "joy of the mountains," and was an herb well-known to the ancients. Today it covers the slopes of Greece, perfuming the air. You can find bunches of dried *rigani* in continental (international) markets. Serves 4–6.

> 1½ *cups yellow button squash cut into wedges or sections*
> 1½ *cups sliced green beans*
> 1½ *cups cauliflower cut into medium-sized florets*
> 1½ *cups broccoli cut into medium-sized florets*
> 1½ *cups zucchini cut into wedges*
> *leaves from a half bunch of silverbeet (Swiss chard), slightly blanched in boiling water and drained*

Lightly cook the vegetables in slightly salted water until just tender. Briefly blanch the silverbeet leaves in the water. Drain all the vegetables thoroughly.

Arrange the hot vegetables on a bed of the slightly blanched silverbeet leaves on a serving platter.

Pour the dressing (recipe follows) on top and serve immediately.

Greek-style Oil-and-Lemon Dressing

> ¼ *cup olive oil*
> 1½ *tbsp lemon juice*
> 2 *teaspoons Greek oregano, or 1 tablespoon fresh oregano leaves, chopped*
> ¼ *teaspoon yellow asafetida powder*
> ¼ *teaspoon salt*
> ¼ *teaspoon freshly ground black pepper*

Combine all ingredients in a screw-top jar, seal, and shake well. Alternatively, combine in a bowl and whisk.

Greek-style Eggplant Casserole (Moussaka)

In my delicious vegetarian counterpart of the famous Greek eggplant-based casserole, the eggplants (aubergines) are first grilled, then layered in a casserole dish with lentils, topped with tasty cheese sauce, and baked. If you wish, the eggplant slices can be deep-fried instead of broiled or grilled, yielding a richer dish. Serves 6.

> 1.5 kg (a little over 3 pounds) eggplants
>   (aubergines), sliced thin
> olive oil

For the lentils

> 2 cups uncooked brown lentils
> 1 tablespoon olive oil
> 1 teaspoon yellow asafetida powder
> 1 cup chopped peeled tomatoes
> 2 tablespoons tomato paste
> 2 teaspoons brown sugar
> 2 teaspoons salt
> ¼ teaspoon black pepper
> 2 tablespoons chopped parsley

For the cheese sauce

> ¼ cup butter
> ⅓ cup flour
> 2 cups milk
> scant ¼ teaspoon nutmeg powder
> ¼ cup grated Parmesan (or Grana Padano) cheese,
>   plus 2 tablespoons for garnish
> ½ teaspoon salt
> ¼ teaspoon black pepper

Prepare eggplant

Preheat griller (broiler) to high. Oil the base of a baking sheet that will fit under the griller. Add a layer of eggplant, and brush the surface of the eggplants with oil. Place them under the hot griller and cook for 5–10 minutes or until lightly golden. Turn the eggplants, brush again with oil, and cook them until lightly golden and soft enough to pierce with a knife point. Remove the cooked eggplants and stack them on a plate. Repeat the grilling until all the eggplant is cooked. Alternatively, deep-fry or pan-fry the eggplant.

Prepare the lentils
Place the uncooked lentils in a 5-liter/quart saucepan over full heat along with 3 or 4 liters of boiling, unsalted water. Bring to a boil, then reduce the heat slightly and cook the lentils until they are soft enough to squeeze between thumb and forefinger. Remove and drain lentils, reserving liquid for soup stock if you wish.

Heat the oil in a saucepan over moderate heat. When oil is hot, sprinkle in asafetida and fry momentarily. Add the tomatoes, increase the heat, and cook for about 5 minutes or until the tomatoes soften and separate from the oil. Stir in the cooked, drained lentils, tomato paste, brown sugar, salt, black pepper, and parsley. Reduce the heat and, stirring when necessary, cook the mixture for about 10 minutes, or until it is fairly dry.

Prepare the cheese sauce
Melt the butter in a 2-liter/quart saucepan over low heat, stir in the flour, and cook over gentle heat for 2 minutes or until the flour changes color slightly. Add the milk, increase the heat, and bring to a boil while stirring constantly. Let the mixture bubble for about 1 minute, then remove the sauce from the heat and whisk in the nutmeg, cheese, salt, and black pepper. Cover the top of the sauce with buttered paper if not using immediately to avoid the sauce forming a skin.

Assemble the dish: Butter a 32.5-cm × 22.5-cm × 5-cm (13 × 9 × 2-inch) oven dish. Place one-third of the eggplant as the base. Top with half the lentils, then add a second layer of eggplant. Spoon on the second layer of lentils, and top with the remaining one-third eggplant. Spread the cheese sauce on top and sprinkle with the remaining cheese.

Bake the casserole in a moderate oven (180°C / 355°F) for 1 hour or until the sauce is slightly golden brown. Allow the moussaka to stand for 10 minutes before cutting into squares and serving.

Nut Pastries in Syrup (Baklava)

Baklava is probably one of the best known of Middle Eastern sweets. In this delightful version, sheets of buttered, wafer-thin filo are layered with nuts and baked. Then they're soaked in a lemon-and-orange-blossom-flavored sugar-and-honey syrup. Makes about 18 large pieces.

Pastries

> 450 g (1 pound) filo pastry (about 30 sheets)
> 1 cup melted unsalted butter
> 250 g (a little more than 1 cup) finely chopped walnuts (or
>   almonds, pistachios, or a combination)
> 1 teaspoon cinnamon powder
> ¼ cup sugar

Syrup

> 1¼ cups sugar
> 1 cup water
> 2 tablespoons lemon juice
> ¼ cup honey
> 1 tablespoon orange-blossom water (available at Middle
>   Eastern grocers)

Butter a 28 × 18-cm (11 × 7-inch) tin. If necessary, cut the filo the size of the tin.

Place one sheet of pastry on the bottom of the tin and butter it with a pastry brush. Repeat for half the pastry (about 15 sheets).

Combine the nuts, cinnamon, and sugar.

Sprinkle the mixture evenly over the top layer of buttered filo. Continue layering the remaining pastry on top of the nut mixture, again brushing each layer of pastry with melted butter. After the final layer of pastry is placed on top, brush it with butter.

Carefully cut the tray of pastry into diagonal diamond shapes with a sharp knife, making sure to cut to the base.

Bake in a moderate oven (180°C / 355°F) for about 45 minutes, or until the top is crisp and golden.

Combine the sugar, water, and lemon juice in a pan, stir over low heat to dissolve the sugar, and then boil for 5 minutes. Remove from the heat, add the honey, stir to dissolve, and add the orange-blossom water.

Pour the hot syrup over the cooked baklava. Let set for at least 2 hours. For best results, leave overnight so that the syrup can be fully absorbed.

Light & Healthy Entertaining

Moghul Cumin Rice (Jeera Pulao)

Moist Vrindavan-style Vegetable and Badi Stew

Malaysian Sweet, Sour and Hot Salad (Rojak)

Baked Polenta Squares with Spicy Tomato Concasse

Grilled Ciabatta with Syrian Roast Pepper and Walnut Dip

Moist and Luscious Maple Fruit Muffins

Moghul Cumin Rice (Jeera Pulao)

This quick to prepare, aromatic rice dish inspired by India's Moghul cuisine is flavored with both whole and ground cumin, and is made even more aromatic by the addition of cloves and cinnamon. The sweet addition of raisins in a savory dish is typical of Moghul taste. Serves 4–6.

> 2¾ cups water
> 2 teaspoons salt
> 2 teaspoons ghee or oil
> 1 teaspoon cumin seeds
> 6 whole cloves
> one 5-cm cinnamon stick
> 2 teaspoons finely chopped fresh ginger
> ½ teaspoon yellow asafetida powder
> 2 teaspoons ground cumin
> 3 tablespoons raisins
> 1½ cups basmati rice
> 3 tablespoons lightly cooked fresh peas or thawed frozen peas

Bring to a boil the water and salt in a small saucepan over moderate heat. Cover with a tight-fitting lid and reduce the heat to low.

Heat the ghee or oil in a larger saucepan over moderate heat. Add the cumin seeds, cloves, and cinnamon stick and toast until the cumin darkens a few shades. Add the ginger, stir-fry until aromatic, then sprinkle in the asafetida, cumin powder, raisins, and rice. Stir the rice for 1–2 minutes or until it turns translucent.

Pour in the water, raise the heat, and quickly bring the rice to a full boil. Stir briefly, then reduce the heat to very low, cover with a tight-fitting lid, and gently simmer without stirring for about 20 minutes or until the grains are tender.

Lift the lid, drop in the peas, and quickly replace the lid. Remove the rice from the heat and set it aside for 5 minutes to allow the rice grains to firm up. Before serving, remove the cinnamon stick and gently fold in the peas. Serve piping hot.

Moist Vrindavan-style Vegetable and Badi Stew

Badi (pronounced "buddy") are sun-dried legume nuggets that add toothsome texture to a variety of dishes. To make *badi*, dried legumes are soaked, drained, wet-ground, seasoned, shaped, and sun-dried until brittle. They can be stored for years, and simply need to be cooked with juicy dishes to reconstitute them. They're full of flavor and packed with fat-free protein. *Badi* (also known as *warian* and *wadi*) can be purchased ready-made at well-stocked Indian groceries. They are also great in pasta sauces and Mexican chili dishes. Serves 6.

   1 tablespoon ghee or oil
   1 cup yellow mung badi, broken into 1.5-cm (½-inch) pieces
   1½ tablespoons grated fresh ginger
   1 teaspoon cumin seeds
   4 medium tomatoes, about 300 g, peeled and chopped
   ½ teaspoon turmeric powder
   ¼ teaspoon cayenne
   3 medium potatoes, about 500 g, peeled and diced
   4–6 cups water
   ¼ cup chopped fresh coriander leaves
   1 teaspoon salt
   ¼ teaspoon black pepper

Heat the ghee or oil over moderate heat in a heavy saucepan. Add *badi* and pan-fry for about 2 minutes or until lightly browned. Remove with a slotted spoon and set aside.

While the saucepan is hot, add the remaining ghee or oil and fry the ginger and cumin for 1–2 minutes or until the cumin darkens a few shades.

Stir in the tomatoes, turmeric, and cayenne. Cook, stirring occasionally, for about 10 minutes or until the tomatoes are pulpy.

Add the fried *badi*, potatoes, 4 cups water, and half the herbs. Bring to a boil, then reduce heat to medium, partially cover, and cook for about 15–20 minutes or until the potatoes are tender. If necessary, add extra water.

Fold in the remaining herbs, salt, and pepper, and set aside for 5 minutes before serving. Serve hot.

Malaysian Sweet, Sour & Hot Salad (Rojak)

The Chinese-Malay salad known as rojak is an example of a classic Indonesian dish (called rujak), a dish that has developed as a hybrid somewhere else. This version tantalizes the senses with a brilliant array of hot, sweet, sour, and salty tastes, coupled with an assortment of juicy, slippery, leafy, crunchy, spongy, and crispy textures. Really, it tastes as good as it sounds. Serves 6.

> ½ large ripe firm pineapple, cut into wedges
> 1 large green mango, peeled, seeded and cut into thin wedges
> 1 choko (chayote), peeled, sliced thin, and lightly salted
> 1 small yam bean (jicama, bangkwang),
>   peeled and cut into wedges
> 2 Lebanese cucumbers cut into wedges
> 100 g fried bean-curd cubes, quartered, or oven-grilled tofu
> leaves from 1 bunch kangkong (water convolvulus),
>   or 1 bunch watercress
> ½ cup roasted peanuts, coarsely ground

Sauce

  2 tablespoons tamarind pulp, reconstituted in ¼ cup water
  2 tablespoons kechap manis (sweet soy sauce)
  2 teaspoons sambal oelek or chopped fresh chillies
  1 teaspoon sweet chili sauce
  1 tablespoon palm sugar, finely ground

Combine sauce ingredients in a bowl and stir to dissolve the sugar.

Serve by arranging the prepared fruits and vegetables, bean curd, and *kangkong* (watercress) leaves on a platter or in individual serving bowls. Drizzle over the sauce and sprinkle with the chopped peanuts. Alternatively, allow each diner to drizzle their own sauce.

Baked Polenta Squares with Spicy Tomato Concasse

Polenta is a fine yellow cornmeal, which after cooking into a thick porridge can be cooled and sliced. In this dish, succulent cubes of cheesy polenta are topped with a tasty herbed tomato purée. Colorful finger food! Makes about 40 squares.

  4 cups water
  1 teaspoon salt
  1¼ cups polenta
  100g (3½ ounces) Parmesan cheese (or Grana Padano)
  spicy tomato concasse (recipe follows)

Boil the salted water, whisk in the polenta, and cook, stirring frequently, over low heat for 10 minutes or until all the liquid is absorbed. Remove from heat and stir in the cheese.

Spoon the polenta into a shallow, oiled 25 × 30-cm (13 × 9-inch) baking dish, spreading it evenly to a thickness of 1 cm (½ inch). Set aside to cool for 10 minutes.

Bake the polenta in an oven set to the highest temperature until crisp and a little golden on top. Remove, cool, and cut into 4 cm (1½-inch) squares.

Serve the polenta squares on a tray, topped with heaped teaspoonfuls of spicy tomato concasse.

Spicy Tomato Concasse
    2 teaspoons olive oil
    1 teaspoon grated fresh ginger
    1 small red chili, seeded and chopped
    ¼ teaspoon yellow asafetida powder
    2 cups chopped, peeled tomatoes
    2 tablespoons chopped kalamata
        olives, or olives of your choice
    1 tablespoon chopped basil leaves
    1 teaspoon sugar
    ½ teaspoon salt

Heat the olive oil in a large, heavy-based saucepan, add the ginger and chili, and cook over low heat for a couple of minutes or until soft. Sprinkle in the asafetida and fry momentarily.

Stir in the tomatoes, bring to a boil, then simmer, stirring occasionally, over low heat for 5 or 10 minutes or until a little reduced.

Add the chopped olives, basil, sugar, and salt, then continue cooking for 5–10 minutes more, or until the mixture becomes a thick purée. Remove from heat. Serve with the cheesy polenta squares.

Grilled Ciabatta with Syrian Roast Pepper and Walnut Dip

There are many versions of the delicious dip known as *muhammara* all over the Middle East. This one is from Syria. *Muhammara's* sourness comes from pomegranate molasses (sometimes called pomegranate concentrate) – a thick, sour, and fruity syrup available from Middle Eastern grocers. Makes 1½ cups dip.

> *2 large red capsicums (peppers)*
> *1 small hot red chili, chopped*
> *1 slice wholemeal (whole-wheat) bread, crusts removed*
> *1 cup shelled walnuts*
> *½ teaspoon yellow asafetida powder*
> *1½ tablespoons pomegranate molasses*
> *juice of ½ lemon*
> *½ teaspoon sugar*
> *½ teaspoon salt*
> *1–3 tablespoons extra virgin olive oil*
> *1 tablespoon flat leaf parsley*
> *toasted ciabatta bread to serve**
> *vegetable crudités to serve (optional)*

Roast the capsicums under a grill (broiler) for 15 minutes or until the skins are blistered and blackened. Place in a plastic bag, seal, and set aside for 5 minutes before peeling. Alternatively, grill the capsicums in the coals of a barbecue.

Combine all ingredients except the parsley, ciabatta, and crudités in a food processor and blend to a thick creamy paste.

Serve sprinkled with parsley and accompanied by chunks of toasted ciabatta and the optional vegetable crudités.

---

* Homebaked bread is both easy and rewarding to make. Look for a recipe that produces a firm, chewy loaf.

Moist and Luscious Maple Fruit Muffins

Our kitchen testing crew couldn't believe it when I disclosed to them that these muffins were completely dairy-free and almost totally fat-free. They are also egg-free, but they are certainly not taste-free, and their texture has to be experienced to be believed. Makes 12 muffins.

>   1 cup pitted semidried California dates, chopped
>   ½ cup maple syrup or mild honey
>   1 teaspoon bicarbonate of soda (baking soda)
>   grated rind and juice of 2 oranges
>   3 green apples, peeled and grated
>   3 cups self-raising wholemeal (whole-wheat) flour
>   1 teaspoon ground cinnamon
>   1 cup sultanas (golden raisins)
>   ½ cup walnuts, chopped
>   low-fat cottage cheese, blended with honey
>   and cinnamon, to serve

Preheat oven to 180°C/350°F.

Combine dates, maple syrup or honey, bicarbonate of soda (baking soda), and 1 cup water in a saucepan. Bring to a boil and simmer over low heat for 2 minutes. Cool to room temperature.

Fold together the remaining ingredients and stir in the date mixture. Mix well and spoon into 12 nonstick muffin tins.

Bake for 25–30 minutes or until the muffins are golden and fully cooked.

Serve the muffins warm or at room temperature with the cottage cheese, honey, and cinnamon.

Vegetarian World Food

Gauranga Potatoes

Crispy Curd Cheese Fritters (Panir Pakoras)

Mung Beans, Rice, and Vegetables (Khichari)

Koftas in Tomato Sauce

Puffed Fried Bread (Poori)

Mixed Vegetables in Creamy Karhi Sauce

Simple Thai Rice

Stuffed Italian Flatbread (Focaccia)

Rich and Tasty Lasagna

with Grilled Vegetables and Sun-dried Tomatoes

Spinach Risotto

Mozzarella and Tomato Pizza

Quick Cherry Cheesecake

Saffron-scented Rice Pudding

Classic Rose Lassi

Gauranga Potatoes

....

Slices of potato folded with herbs, butter, and sour cream and then baked to a golden brown: irresistibly rich and delicious, yet effortless to prepare. Serves 4–6.

> 8 medium potatoes, peeled and sliced
> 1 tablespoon olive oil
> ¾ teaspoon yellow asafetida powder
> ½ teaspoon ground dried rosemary
> ¼ teaspoon freshly ground black pepper
> ½ teaspoon turmeric
> 2–3 cups light sour cream
> 1 tablespoon melted butter
> 2 teaspoons salt
> ½ cup water
> 1 teaspoon sweet paprika
> 2 tablespoons chopped fresh parsley

Boil the potato slices in lightly salted water in a 4-liter/quart saucepan until they are cooked but firm. Remove and drain.

Heat the olive oil in a medium saucepan over moderate heat and, when hot, add the asafetida. Sauté momentarily. Add the rosemary, black pepper, and turmeric and stir briefly. Add the sour cream, melted butter, salt, and water. Whisk it into a smooth sauce and remove from the heat.

Combine the potato slices and sour cream sauce in a mixing bowl. Pour the mixture into a casserole dish, sprinkle with paprika, and place in the top of a preheated 200°C/390°F oven.

Bake for 30 minutes or until the top is golden brown. Garnish with fresh parsley.

Serve hot.

Crispy Curd-Cheese Fritters (Panir Pakoras)

Homemade curd cheese is easy to make and is irresistible when batter-fried crispy on the outside and smooth and creamy on the inside. Serve hot panir pakoras with a wedge of lemon or lime and a spoonful of tamarind chutney (see page 74). The curd should be homemade, pressed under a heavy weight, cut up while still hot and slightly moist, immediately cooked in the batter, and served hot. You can use the same batter recipe for a variety of vegetables. Try dipping chunks of cauliflower, slices of potato, broccoli florets, eggplant, etc. (For a spicier batter, add one or more of the following: 1 tsp cumin powder, 2 tsp coriander powder, and ½–1 tsp chili powder.) Serves 6–8.

fresh curd cheese (panir) from 2 liters milk (see recipe on
page 69)
⅓ cup chickpea flour
⅓ cup plain (white) flour
⅓ cup self-raising flour
2 teaspoons salt
1 teaspoon yellow asafetida powder
¼ teaspoon turmeric
1½ teaspoons green chilies, minced
1 cup cold water, or as required
ghee or oil for deep-frying

Whisk together the flours, salt, spices, and chilies in a bowl and add cold water to form a thick batter. Let stand for 10 minutes.

Remove the weight from the freshly prepared curd cheese and, while the cheese is still hot, cut it into 1.5-cm (¾-inch) cubes or 3.75-cm (1½-inch) long strips.

Heat ghee or oil in a wok or deep-frying pan until fairly hot (180°C/355°F).

Dip 6 or 7 pieces of curd in the batter and carefully lower them into the hot oil one at a time. The temperature will fall. Adjust the heat to maintain frying temperature. Cook the pakoras, turning occasionally, until they are golden brown all over (about 4–5 minutes).

Remove with a slotted spoon and drain on paper towels. Cook all the pakoras in the same manner and serve hot.

Mung Beans, Rice, and Vegetables (Khichari)

Khichari (pronounced "kitch-eri") is an important dish for vegetarians. The flavorsome, juicy stew of mung beans, rice, and vegetables is both nutritious and sustaining. It can be served any time a one-pot meal is required. Serve it accompanied by a little yogurt, some whole-wheat toast, lemon or lime wedges, and topped with a drizzle of melted ghee (if desired). Bliss! Serves 4–6.

½ cup split mung beans, washed and drained
6 cups water
1 bay leaf
thumb-size chunk ginger, chopped fine
1 small green chili, seeded and chopped
½ teaspoon turmeric
2 teaspoons coriander powder
1 cup basmati rice or other long-grain rice of your choice
1 packed cup each broccoli, potato cubes, and quartered
*   Brussels sprouts, or vegetables of your choice*
2 ripe tomatoes, chopped
1½ teaspoons salt
3 teaspoons ghee or oil
2 teaspoons cumin seeds
small handful curry leaves

½ teaspoon yellow asafetida powder
½ cup chopped fresh coriander leaves
wedges of lemon, some chilled yogurt, and extra ghee
   (if desired) for serving

Bring to a boil the mung beans, water, bay leaf, ginger, chili, turmeric, and coriander in a saucepan, then reduce to a simmer and cook, partially covered, for about 15 minutes or until the beans start to break down.

Add the rice, vegetables, tomatoes, and salt, increase the heat, and stirring, bring to a boil, then return to a simmer, covered. Stirring occasionally, cook for another 10–15 minutes, or until the rice is soft.

Season: Heat the ghee in a small saucepan over moderate heat. Sprinkle in the cumin seeds, fry until they darken a few shades, then add the curry leaves. Sprinkle in the asafetida, swirl the pan, and empty the fried seasonings into the *khichari*. Stir the seasonings through, then return the *khichari* to a simmer and cook for another 5 minutes or so, or until the rice is fully swollen and soft. If you desire a moist *khichari*, add a little boiling water now.

Fold in the fresh coriander, and serve the *khichari* piping hot with a drizzle of warm ghee if desired, and the accompaniments suggested above.

Koftas in Tomato Sauce

Koftas are succulent, Indian-style vegetable balls that can be served soaking in sauce or smothered in gravy. A number of vegetables are suitable for making kofta – potato, cabbage, cauliflower, spinach, and radish being the most popular. Makes 24 koftas.

Sauce

- 2 teaspoons olive oil
- 2 teaspoons butter (optional)
- 2 bay leaves
- ½ teaspoon yellow asafetida powder
- 4 cups tomato purée
- 1 teaspoon dried basil
- 2 teaspoons salt
- ¼ teaspoon freshly ground black pepper
- 1½ teaspoons sugar

Koftas

- 2 cups grated cauliflower
- 2 cups grated cabbage
- 1½ cups chickpea flour
- ½ teaspoon yellow asafetida powder
- 1 teaspoon ground cumin
- 1½ teaspoon salt
- 1 teaspoon garam masala
- ½ teaspoon cayenne
- ghee or oil for deep-frying

Prepare the sauce

Heat the oil and optional butter together in a saucepan over moderate heat. When hot, drop in the bay leaves and sauté for 1 minute or until fragrant. Sprinkle in the yellow asafetida powder and fry momentarily.

Stir in the tomato purée and basil. Raise the heat, bring to a boil, then reduce the heat and simmer for 10 minutes or until a little reduced.

Add the salt, pepper, and sugar. Remove from the heat and keep warm.

Prepare the Koftas

Combine all kofta ingredients in a bowl until well mixed. Roll the mixture into 24 balls. Heat the ghee or oil for deep-frying in a wok or deep pan over fairly high heat (180°C/350°F). Carefully drop in 6–8 balls.

Fry the koftas for 2–3 minutes or until they rise to the surface and start to color. Reduce the heat to low and fry for another 8–10 minutes or until they are a deep reddish brown. Remove and drain on paper towels. Reheat the oil to its original temperature, and repeat the frying procedure for the remaining batches of kofta.

Soak the koftas in the hot sauce 10 minutes before serving to allow them to become plump and succulent. They are great on a bed of steaming hot rice or couscous as part of a main meal. They also work well as an accompaniment to other dishes.

Puffed Fried Bread (Puri)

Puris are traditional Indian fried breads made with straight wholemeal (whole-wheat) flour, but you can vary the ingredients. One-half wholemeal or *atta*, and one-half unbleached plain (white) flour makes lighter puris. If you're expert at rolling, try using only plain (white) flour for translucent, gossamer-thin puris.

Puris are traditionally eaten hot, but cold puris are great for picnics or snacks when traveling. Serve puris with practically any menu at any time. Makes 16 medium-sized puris.

2 cups sifted chapati flour (atta) or half-wholemeal (whole-wheat) and half-unbleached plain (white)
½ teaspoon salt
2 tablespoons melted butter, ghee, or oil
⅔ cup warm water, or as needed
ghee or oil for deep-frying

Combine the flour and salt in a mixing bowl. Rub in the butter or ghee until the mixture resembles coarse meal. Add up to ⅔ cup water, slowly pouring in just enough to form a medium-soft, kneadable dough. Turn the dough onto a clean working surface.

Knead the dough for 5–8 minutes or until silky smooth. Cover with an overturned bowl and let rest for ½–3 hours.

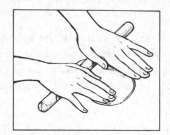

Reknead the dough again for 1 minute. Divide the dough into 16 portions, roll each portion into a smooth ball, and cover all the balls with a damp cloth.

Preheat ghee or oil in a wok or deep pan over low heat. Meanwhile, with a rolling pin, roll all your balls of dough into smooth disks about 11.5 cm (4½ inches) wide. Increase the ghee or oil temperature until it reaches about 185°C/365°F.

Lift up a rolled puri and slip it into the hot oil, making sure it doesn't fold over. It will sink to the bottom, then immediately rise to the surface. Hold it under the surface with a slotted spoon until it puffs up into a balloon. Let it brown slightly to a golden color, then turn it over and cook the other side to the same even golden colour. Lift out the puri with the slotted spoon and carefully drain it in a large colander.

Repeat for all the puris. Serve immediately, if possible, or leave in a preheated, slightly warm oven for up to 2 hours.

Mixed Vegetables in Creamy Karhi Sauce

Karhis are smooth, yogurt-based dishes served with rice. Either yogurt or buttermilk is whisked with chickpea flour and then simmered into a creamy sauce. *Karhi* is an excellent source of vegetarian protein. *Karhis* are delicious, light, easy to digest, and good for you. What more could you ask! Serves 6.

1½ cups carrots, peeled and cut into chunks
1½ cups green beans, cut into short lengths
1½ cups small cauliflower florets
1½ cups green peas
2 cups plain yogurt
½ cup chickpea flour (besan)
2½ cups water
1 teaspoon chili powder
½ teaspoon turmeric powder
1 teaspoon coriander powder
2 teaspoons ghee or oil
1 teaspoon brown mustard seeds
1½ teaspoons cumin seeds
1 teaspoon yellow asafetida powder
1½ teaspoons salt
2 tablespoons chopped fresh coriander leaves

Steam all the vegetables until just tender, drain, cover, and set aside.

Whisk together the yogurt with the chickpea flour until smooth and creamy. Add the water, chili powder, turmeric, and coriander, and whisk again.

Heat the ghee or oil in a medium saucepan over moderate heat. When it's fairly hot, sprinkle in the mustard seeds, and fry them until they crackle. Add the cumin, fry until it darkens a few shades, then drop in the asafetida and fry momentarily.

Pour in the yogurt mixture, and stirring, bring to a boil. Reduce the heat and simmer for 10 minutes, stirring occasionally.

Fold in the steamed vegetables, salt, and fresh coriander. Serve hot with rice.

Simple Thai Rice

Thai Jasmine rice is an aromatic long-grain rice from Thailand. Serve it as an accompaniment to Chinese or South East Asian savory or vegetable dishes. Serves 3–4.

> 1½ cups Thai rice
> 2½ cups water
> salt (optional)

Bring to a boil the water and optional salt in a 2-liter/quart saucepan over moderate heat.

Add the rice, raise the heat, and allow the water to return to a boil. Reduce heat and allow rice to gently simmer, covered with a tight-fitting lid. Cook rice without stirring for 15 minutes. Remove the rice from the heat, leaving it covered for another 5 minutes before serving. Serve hot.

Stuffed Italian Flatbread (Focaccia)

Focaccia has become a national dish of Italy, and many regional versions can be found. This version is probably a cross between the local country cuisine of the Puglia region, where breads are enriched with the ingredients of the pastoral people – tomatoes, herbs, and oil – and those southern versions adding cheese. This recipe makes a large, thick focaccia (it can only *just* be called a "flat bread") filled with a variety of tasty, herby, melty, mouth-watering ingredients. Serve focaccia hot from the oven. Makes 1 thick, 25-cm (10-inch) bread.

Dough

3 teaspoons dried yeast
1 cup warm water
½ teaspoon sugar
3 cups unbleached plain (white) bread flour
1 teaspoon yellow asafetida powder
½ teaspoon salt
4 tablespoons olive oil

Filling

2 cups grated cheddar cheese
2 cups grated mozzarella cheese
½ cup freshly grated Parmesan cheese (or Grana Padano)
½ –¾ cup halved or chopped kalamata olives
packed ½ cup coarsely chopped
    oil-packed sun-dried tomatoes
packed ½ cup chopped fresh basil leaves
1–2 tablespoons oil from sun-dried tomatoes
½ teaspoon freshly ground black pepper

Topping

a little olive oil for brushing on the bread
dried basil for sprinkling
coarse sea salt (optional)

Stir the dried yeast into ¼ cup of the warm water. Sprinkle in the sugar and leave in a warm place for about 10 minutes, or until frothy.

Sift the flour, asafetida, and salt into a large bowl. Pour in the frothy yeast mixture, the olive oil, and the remaining water. Mix well.

Knead on a floured surface for 8–10 minutes or until the dough is velvety soft. Place the dough in a lightly oiled bowl and cover the bowl with oiled plastic wrap. Leave the dough in a warm, draft-free place for about 45 minutes, or until doubled in size.

Punch the dough down and remove it from the bowl. Place it on a lightly floured surface and knead it briefly. Divide the dough into two equal portions. Roll out one portion to a 25-cm (10-inch) disk and place it on a well-oiled baking sheet.

Sprinkle on half the cheeses, leaving a 1.25-cm (½-inch) border of dough. Evenly cover the cheese with the olives, sun-dried tomatoes, and basil leaves. Drizzle over the oil from the sun-dried tomatoes, and sprinkle on the black pepper. Cover with the remaining cheese. Moisten the outer border of exposed dough with water.

Preheat the oven to 220°C/430°F.

Roll out the other portion of dough to exactly the same size and carefully place it on top of the filled base. Tightly seal top and bottom, making sure no filling is exposed. Brush the surface of the focaccia with olive oil, and sprinkle with basil and the optional sea salt. Place the focaccia in the center of the oven.

Bake for 30 minutes or until top is golden brown. Remove and carefully place the bread on a rack to cool, or cut into wedges and serve immediately.

Note: For variety, try adding one or more of the following fillings: 1–2 cups thinly-sliced grilled or pan-fried zucchini, 1–2 cups steamed or pan-fried tender asparagus, 1–2 cups capsicum strips, 1–2 cups grilled or pan-fried eggplant slices, 1–2 cups marinated artichoke hearts.

Rich and Tasty Lasagna with Grilled Vegetables and Sun-dried Tomatoes

I allowed my imagination to run wild when I constructed this multi-layered deep-dish lasagna. You might like to substitute different vegetables in some of the layers. Thin slices of butternut squash or zucchini slices can be successfully grilled and added. Select a casserole dish 25 × 35 × 8 cm (10 × 14 × 3 inch) for this "queen of lasagna." Makes 1 deep-dish lasagna.

Vegetables

1 large eggplant (aubergine) sliced into thin rings and grilled
3 large red capsicums (peppers) cut into quarters lengthwise,
    cored, de-veined, and grilled
leaves from ½ large bunch English spinach, stalks removed
½ cup sun-dried tomatoes sliced into strips

Tomato Sauce

¼ cup olive oil
½ teaspoon yellow asafetida powder
1 cup fresh basil, chopped
2 teaspoons dried oregano
6 cups tomato purée
1 teaspoon salt
¼ teaspoon black pepper
1 teaspoon raw or brown sugar
2 tablespoons tomato paste

Bechamel Sauce

    125 g (6–7 tablespoons) butter
    ¼ teaspoon nutmeg powder
    ¼ teaspoon black pepper
    ½ cup plain flour
    4 cups warmed milk

Cheeses

    3½ cups grated cheddar cheese
    2 cups grated mozzarella cheese
    ½ cup grated Parmesan cheese (or Grano Padano)
        plus 3 tablespoons reserved

Pasta

    500 g (a little over 1 pound) instant lasagna noodles

Prepare the tomato sauce

Pour the olive oil into a large, heavy-based saucepan and set over moderate heat. When the oil is hot, sprinkle in the asafetida, fry momentarily, then add the basil and oregano and fry for another 30 seconds. Pour in the puréed tomatoes, stir to mix, and bring to a boil. Add the salt, black pepper, sugar, and tomato paste, reduce the heat slightly, and cook uncovered, stirring often for 10–15 minutes or until it reduces and thickens.

Prepare the bechamel sauce

Melt the butter in a 2-liter/quart heavy saucepan over low heat. Stir in the nutmeg, black pepper, and flour, and fry, stirring constantly, for about half a minute or until the mixture loosens. Remove the saucepan from the heat and gradually pour in the warm milk, stirring with a whisk until it is incorporated and the sauce is smooth. Return the sauce to moderate heat and bring to a boil, stirring. Reduce the heat and simmer for about 5 minutes, stirring constantly, until the sauce develops a thick, custardlike consistency.

Assemble the lasagna

Combine all three cheeses (except the reserved Parmesan). Divide the cheese into 2 portions, the tomato sauce into 3 portions, the bechamel sauce into 4 portions, and the pasta into 5.

Spread one portion of the tomato sauce on the bottom of the ovenproof casserole dish. Place a portion of the pasta on top. Layer the eggplant slices on top of the pasta. Spread on a portion of the bechamel sauce, then another of the pasta. Sprinkle on half the grated cheese.

Continue layering as follows: a portion of the tomato sauce, sun-dried tomatoes, capsicum slices, pasta, bechamel, pasta, and the remaining cheese. Layer the spinach leaves on top of the cheese.

Spread the remaining tomato sauce on top, top with the last pasta and remaining double portion of bechamel (this white-sauce layer needs to be thicker than the others). Sprinkle the top with the reserved Parmesan. Place the lasagna in the top half of a preheated 200°C/390°F oven.

Bake for 45–60 minutes or until the top is slightly golden and the pasta yields easily to a knife point. If the lasagna is darkened on top but does not yield fully to a knife point, cover the lasagna with brown paper or aluminum foil in the last 15 minutes of cooking. When the lasagna is done, leave it in the oven with the door ajar for at least 30 minutes to allow the lasagna to "plump" up and set. Cut and serve as required.

Spinach Risotto

Risotto is one of my favorite ways to eat rice. I love its firm, slightly sticky feel in my mouth, and its wonderful buttery opulence. Spinach looks very appealing in risotto, and tastes good too. Serves 6.

6–7 cups light vegetable stock
250 g (about half a pound) spinach leaves
2 tablespoons butter or olive oil
½ teaspoon yellow asafetida powder
2 cups arborio rice
1 teaspoon salt
big pinch nutmeg
1 cup freshly grated Parmesan (or Grana Padano) cheese
3 tablespoons extra Parmesan (or Grana Padano) reserved
    for sprinkling

Bring to a boil the vegetable stock in a medium saucepan over full heat. Add the spinach and blanch for 1 minute. Lower the heat under the stock. Remove the spinach with a slotted spoon. Squeeze the water from the spinach, returning the water to the simmering stock.

Finely chop the spinach and set it aside.

Melt 2 tablespoons of the butter in a large, heavy saucepan over a fairly low heat. Sprinkle in the asafetida, stir momentarily, and add the rice.

Stir the rice in the flavored butter for 1–2 minutes to coat it.

Ladle in ½ cup simmering stock. Gently stir the rice and stock. When the stock is absorbed, add another ½ cup. When half the stock has been used, add the spinach to the rice. Continue adding stock and gently stirring the rice until there is no more stock to add. The finished rice should be creamy in texture, neither soupy nor dry.

Fold the salt, nutmeg, remaining butter, and Parmesan cheese into the rice and stir through.

Serve the risotto with a garnish of reserved Parmesan.

Mozzarella and Tomato Pizza

A crisp-crusted pizza holding a filling of herb-flavored tomatoes with a topping of sliced black olives, peppers, and golden, melt-ing mozzarella – yum! To save time, prepare the filling while the dough is rising. Makes one 25-cm (10-inch) pizza.

Base

3 teaspoons fresh yeast
½ teaspoon sugar
½ cup lukewarm water
1½ cups plain (white) flour
¼ teaspoon salt
2 tablespoons olive oil

Filling

2 teaspoons olive oil
¼ teaspoon yellow asafetida powder
one 400 g (14-ounce) can whole Italian tomatoes, chopped
    and undrained, or 1½ cups fresh tomato purée
1 tablespoon tomato paste
½ teaspoon dried oregano
½ teaspoon dried basil
1 teaspoon sugar
1 teaspoon salt
¼ teaspoon freshly ground black pepper

Topping

¾ cup grated mozzarella cheese
2 tablespoons grated Parmesan (or Grana Padano) cheese
1 cup thin strips of eggplant, deep-fried until
    dark golden-brown, then salted
1 small red pepper, diced
¼ cup black olives, pitted and halved

Cream the yeast with the sugar in a bowl, add lukewarm water, and let stand for 10 minutes or until bubbles appear on the surface.

Sift flour and salt into a bowl, make a well in the center, and add the oil and yeast mixture. Mix to a firm dough. Turn out the dough onto a floured surface and knead for 10 minutes or until the dough is smooth and elastic. Place dough in a lightly oiled bowl, cover, and leave in a warm place for 30 minutes or until the dough has doubled in size.

Punch down the dough with your fist and knead into a small ball. Flatten the dough with a rolling pin and roll into a circular sheet of pastry that will just fit a 25-cm (10-inch) pizza pan. Place the dough carefully on the pan.

Prepare your filling: Heat the olive oil in a large frying pan over moderate heat. When hot, add the asafetida and sauté momentarily. Add the undrained canned tomatoes or tomato purée, tomato paste, oregano, basil, sugar, salt, and pepper. Bring the sauce to a boil, then reduce the heat, and stirring occasionally, simmer uncovered for 10–15 minutes or until the sauce is thick and smooth. Allow the filling to cool somewhat.

Spread cooled filling over pizza base, leaving a little border uncovered. Combine half the grated mozzarella cheese with the Parmesan and sprinkle over the tomato filling. Top with the eggplant strips, chopped peppers, and olives. Sprinkle on the remaining cheese.

Bake in a preheated hot oven (220°C/430°F) for 15–20 minutes or until the crust is golden brown.

Serve hot.

Quick Cherry Cheesecake

This delectable, attractive cheesecake requires no baking. It features a biscuit-crumb base and a filling of cream cheese folded with plump, sour cherries. Makes one 20 cm (8-inch) cheesecake.

> *180 g (8 ounces) fairly plain sweet biscuits (cookies)**
> *100 g (5 tablespoons) butter, chopped*
> *1 teaspoon bitter almond extract (optional)*
> *one 400-g (14-ounce) tin sweetened condensed milk*
> *½ cup freshly squeezed lemon juice*
> *1 teaspoon pure vanilla extract*
> *250 g (8 ounces) cream cheese, chopped*
> *1 tablespoon cornflour (cornstarch)*
> *1¼ cups sour cherries in syrup, drained well*
> *¼ cup sour cherries, plus ½ cup syrup reserved for topping*

Prepare the base
Process the biscuits in a food processor until reduced to a fine powder. Drop in the butter and the bitter almond extract, if using. Process until mixture is fully blended. Remove the mixture and press it evenly into the base and up the sides of a prebuttered 20-cm (8-inch) fluted pie tin.

Prepare the filling
Add the condensed milk, lemon juice, vanilla, and cream cheese to the food processor and blend until smooth. Remove the mix to a bowl. Fold in the 1¼ cups drained sour cherries. Pour the mixture into the prepared crust.

Prepare the topping
Combine the cornflour (cornstarch) with a couple of teaspoons

---

* Baking your biscuits for the crust of this cheesecake allows you to create interesting flavor combinations. For example, try adding ground almonds or pecans to the cookie dough.

of cherry syrup to make a runny paste. Combine with the remaining syrup and reserved sour cherries in a small saucepan, and stirring, bring to a boil over moderate heat. When the mixture thickens, quickly pour it over the top of the cheesecake and spread as desired.

Chill the cheesecake for at least 3 hours before removing from its base. Serve. (But the cheesecake is at its best the next day.)

(To speed up setting time, place the cheesecake [before you add the cherry topping] in a prewarmed 175°C/345°F oven for 10 minutes. Remove, top with the cherry topping, and chill for 2 hours.

Saffron-scented Rice Pudding

This is an Indian dish called *chaval kshira*. *Kshira* is Sanskrit for condensed milk. It is commonly known as kheer in North India, and regional variations are known as *payasa* or *payesh*. When milk is slowly condensed with rice, the result is this creamy dessert, more simply known as "sweet rice." Serves 4–5.

> *½ cup short-grain rice*
> *big pinch pure saffron threads*
> *7 cups fresh whole milk*
> *¾ cup sugar*

Clean, wash, and drain the short-grain rice. Pour the milk into a heavy 5- or 6-quart saucepan. Sprinkle in the saffron threads. Stirring constantly with a wooden spoon, bring the milk to the boil over moderately high heat. Reduce the heat, add the rice, and still stirring attentively, boil gently for 25–30 minutes.

Reduce the heat to moderately low and boil the milk for another 10–15 minutes, still stirring constantly with a smooth, sweeping action. When the sweet rice becomes creamy and slightly thick, remove the pan from the heat. Stir in the sugar, mix well, and allow the sweet rice to cool slightly and serve warm. Alternatively, refrigerate for at least 3 hours and serve chilled.

Note: If the sweet rice thickens too much after it cools, add a little cold milk or light cream to thin it out.

Classic Rose Lassi

My first taste of *lassi* was in New Delhi on a dusty, blistering hot day in 1978. A friend and I took shelter in a tiny shop somewhere in Chandni Chowk Bazaar and were transported to a refrigerated heaven the moment the smooth, frothy, icy-cold rose-flavored yogurt beverage touched our lips. Serves 4.

> 2½ cups plain yogurt
> ½ cup fine sugar
> 2 teaspoons pure distilled rosewater (I prefer Lebanese)
> ¾ cup ice water
> 1 cup ice cubes, cracked
> a few fragrant rose petals for garnish, optional

Process the yogurt, sugar, rosewater, and ice water in a blender for 2 minutes. Add the ice and process for another 2 minutes.

Serve in tall, refrigerated glasses with a garnish of rose petals. Chill out!

Glossary of Ingredients

Asafetida – An aromatic resin, also known as *hing*, used in cooking to replace onions and garlic. To cook with asafetida, small quantities of the powdered form are sautéed in a small amount of warm oil or ghee before adding to savory dishes. I recommend the mild Vandevi brand of yellow asafetida powder over the gray variety. All recipes in this book using asafetida were tested using Vandevi asafetida. If using another brand, reduce the quantity to between a quarter and a half of the suggested amount. It is available in well-stocked health food stores and in Indian and Asian markets.

Basmati Rice – a light-textured, long-grain aromatic rice from North India and Pakistan, with a wonderful fragrance and flavor. I have found Dehradun basmati to be superior. Basmati rice is available at Indian, Middle Eastern, and Asian grocers, and at well-stocked supermarkets.

Bok Choy – Chinese cabbage. These small cabbages have dark green leaves and wide, white stalks that are joined near the base of the stem and resemble miniature Swiss chards (silverbeets). The smaller the individual cabbage, the more delicate the flavor. Bok choy is available at many supermarkets, farmers' markets, and Chinese grocers.

Bulgur Wheat – made by parboiling and drying whole wheat kernels and then crushing them into various sizes. It has a chewy texture and a pleasant nutty taste, and is rich in protein, calcium, phosphorus, and iron. Bulgur wheat is available at health food stores and Middle Eastern grocers, as well as in the specialty aisles of well-stocked supermarkets.

Cardamom – The aromatic seeds of the fruit of the tropical plant *Elettaria cardamomum*. The odor and flavor of cardamom is reminiscent of lemon rind and eucalyptus. Cardamom is popular in Middle Eastern dishes. In Indian cuisine, it is used in rice, milk sweets, and halava. It is also chewed as a breath freshener and digestive aid after a meal. Cardamom is available in the pod (green or bleached), as seeds, or powdered. I would suggest you purchase whole pods and shell the seeds yourself. Shop at Indian or Middle Eastern groceries for the freshest cardamom.

Cayenne Pepper – The orange-red to deep-red powder derived from small, sun-dried, pungent red chili peppers. Use carefully – it's hot! – to add zest and flavor to dishes. Used in Mexican and Indian cuisine, and available from supermarkets and well-stocked grocers.

Chickpea Flour – A finely milled flour made from ground, roasted *chana* dal. It is popular in Indian cuisine in batters, as a binding agent, and in confectionery. Also known as *besan*, gram flour, and garbanzo flour, it is available at Indian grocers.

Chickpeas – Known as garbanzo beans in Spanish cuisine and *ceci* in Italian. Chickpeas must be soaked before cooking, then boiled until soft. Used extensively in world cuisines, they are available in many supermarkets and at international, Indian, and Middle Eastern grocers.

Chilies – There are hundreds of varieties of chilies ranging in strength from sweet to fiery hot. The seeds and inner white ribs of chilies are the hottest parts, and recipes often call for removing both to tame the heat.

Chinese Black Beans – Soybeans fermented with malt and salt and having a strong, salty flavor. They are popular in Chinese and Indonesian cooking, especially as the basis for black bean sauce. Not to be mistaken for the large black shiny beans that share the same name, Chinese black beans are available at Chinese and Southeast Asian grocers.

Choy Sum – Also known as rape, the seeds of which are the source of rapeseed oil. A common, delicately flavored vegetable used in Chinese and Japanese cuisine. Available at Chinese groceries year round.

Coconut Milk – Also called *santan* in Indonesian cooking. Coconut milk is extracted from fresh coconut pulp and used in Southeast Asian, Indian, and Indonesian dishes. Available in cans from supermarkets and Asian grocers.

Coriander Leaves – Also called cilantro, coriander is the most common flavoring herb in the world, on a par with parsley. It is found in supermarkets and international food stores.

Coriander Seeds – Coriander seeds are a favorite flavoring spice in Indian, Greek, and some Latin American cuisines. Coriander is available whole or ground, although I recommend purchasing whole seeds and grinding them yourself. Coriander seeds are available at Indian and Middle Eastern groceries and well-stocked supermarkets.

Couscous – Made from semolina. Most common and widely known in North African and Arab dishes. Available at well-stocked supermarkets and Middle Eastern groceries.

Cumin Seeds – Cumin seeds have a warm, aromatic, and slightly bitter flavor and are used extensively in Indian, Middle Eastern, and Latin American cuisines. The flavor and aroma emerges best after dry-roasting and then adding the seeds to hot oil. Available at any Indian or Middle Eastern grocer, and many well-stocked supermarkets.

Curry Leaves – Curry leaves are highly aromatic when fresh. Used especially in South Indian kitchens, they are generally sautéed in oil with mustard seeds and asafetida and added to dals, chutneys, or vegetable dishes. Available in Indian groceries.

Fennel Seeds – Fennel seeds are especially used in Indian cuisine. They have an agreeably sweet fragrance similar to anise and are used in a variety of vegetable dishes, dals, and pastries. The seeds are available at well-stocked supermarkets and Indian grocers.

Garam Masala – A blend of dry-roasted and ground spices well-used in Indian cuisine. The spices warm the body and include dried chilies, black pepper, cardamom, coriander, cinnamon, cloves, and cumin (although there are other recipes depending on the region). Garam masala is added toward the end of cooking. It can be purchased at Indian groceries and well-stocked supermarkets.

Ginger – Fresh ginger root has a spicy, sweet aroma and a hot, clean taste, and is used in many cuisines. Young, "green" ginger is especially appreciated for its fiber-free texture and mild flavor. Mature ginger root is more readily available at produce markets, Asian groceries, and many supermarkets. Ginger powder is not a substitute for fresh ginger, because it has lost its volatile essential oils and is sometimes stale or adulterated. Ginger powder is used mostly in European cooking and in baking. Ginger powder is available at most groceries and supermarkets.

Grana Padano – A cheese in the tradition of grana or hard, slightly sweet, crumbly, mature Italian cheeses. As with any cheese, be sure to read the label to avoid animal-based rennet.

Kalamata Olives – Large, ink-black olives with pointed ends and shiny skins, named after the seaside town in southern Greece where they are grown. Popular in Greek cuisine, they are flavorsome and full-bodied. Available in well-stocked supermarkets and in international groceries.

Kaffir Lime – Not a true lime, but the fruit of the Southeast Asian tree *Citrus hystrix*. Although the fruit, which is used when it is still immature, has little juice, the rind and leaves are a popular addition to curries, soups, and salads. It is also known as *makrut* lime. Available at Southeast Asian grocers.

Lemon Grass – Lemon grass is one of the most popular herbs in Southeast Asia and is usually sold in a bundle of three or four stems devoid of leaves. Look for firm, wrinkle-free stems. The bulbous lower stem, creamy white to pale green, is the part to use. If lemon grass is not available, substitute two or three strips of thinly peeled lemon zest per stalk of lemon grass.

Mung Beans – Protein-rich, green-skinned whole oval beans commonly used for sprouting. Whole green mung beans are excellent for stews and soups as well as for Indian dry-bean dishes. They are available at Indian or Asian grocers or at specialty stores. Split, they are known as mung dal and are a popular food item in Indian cuisine. Available at Indian or Asian groceries.

Mustard Seeds – The mustard seeds used in this book are the tiny round brown seeds from the plant *Brassica juncea*, commonly used in Indian cuisine. Available at Indian groceries.

Pine Nuts – Also known as pine kernels, pignolia, or pinoli, pine nuts have a delicious, delicate, nutty taste and are popular in Italian, Spanish, and Middle Eastern cuisine. Available at well-stocked supermarkets and at specialty, international, or Middle Eastern groceries.

Rose Water – The diluted essence of rose petals, particularly from the highly scented varieties, *Rosa damascena* and *Rosa centifolia*. Available at Middle Eastern and Indian grocers.

Sorrel – Sorrel, which is in the rhubarb family, has a refreshing, somewhat bitter, sour, spinachlike flavor. It should always be cooked for a minimum time to preserve its fresh flavor. If used raw in salads, select only young, tender leaves. Available at well-stocked supermarkets and at farmers' markets and specialty stores.

Tahini – A sesame butter used in Middle Eastern cuisine with the consistency of runny peanut butter, tahini is the basis of various salad dressings and sauces. Available in supermarkets and at Middle Eastern, specialty, and international markets.

Tamarind – The pulp extracted from the brown pods of the tamarind tree. The fresh pulp has a sour, fruity taste and is popular in Indian and Indonesian cooking. Available in blocks or as concentrate, tamarind makes excellent sweet-and-sour chutneys or sauces and can be used in vegetable dishes and curries. Tamarind in its various forms is available at Indian and Southeast Asian groceries.

Thai (Jasmine) Rice – A long-grained aromatic white rice from Thailand. It cooks to large, soft, fluffy grains. Available at well-stocked supermarkets and at Asian groceries.

Tofu – Used in Chinese, Japanese, Korean, and Indonesian cooking, this white, almost tasteless and odorless curd is produced from soybeans that have been successively crushed, boiled in water, strained, and pressed into a mold. Tofu is sold fresh in most Chinese grocers, but is now available in many supermarkets, health food stores, and specialty shops.

Turmeric – Powdered turmeric is a fine, aromatic, yellowish powder and an essential ingredient in Asian and especially Indian cooking. Turmeric adds a brilliant yellow color to cooked dishes and imparts a slightly bitter, pungent flavor. Available in well-stocked supermarkets and at Indian groceries.

Vietnamese Mint – This pungent herb is not a true mint. It is also known as Cambodian Mint, hot mint, *laksa* leaf, *daun laksa*, and *daun kesom* and is easily available from Vietnamese grocers, where it is known as *rau ram*. The leaves are narrow and pointed, with distinctive dark markings in the center. In Vietnamese cooking, the herb is not cooked but is used in salads or eaten as a fresh accompaniment to Vietnamese spring rolls.

Concluding Words

The careful preparation and profuse public distribution of *pra-sāda* (vegetarian foods offered to Lord Kṛṣṇa) has always been an essential element of the Vedic culture. Since 1966, devotees of the International Society for Krishna Consciousness (ISKCON) have followed this tradition by serving out over 150 million nourishing free multicourse dinners, opening over thirty vegetarian restaurants, founding over thirty vegetarian farm communities, and widely publicizing the value of a spiritual vegetarian diet through books, magazines, and films. Also, many followers of the Kṛṣṇa religion have begun various *prasāda* businesses, producing a wide variety of healthy, nutritious, natural foods. All this makes the International Society for Krishna Consciousness – unique in its spiritual approach to diet – the strongest and most well organized force for vegetarianism in the world today.

The Sunday Feast

The founder-*ācārya* (spiritual master) of the Hare Kṛṣṇa movement, Śrīla Prabhupāda, started the now-famous Sunday feasts in 1966. At the first Kṛṣṇa temple in the Western world, located in New York's Lower East Side, he would personally help cook the twelve-course meals. Regular attendance at the feast rapidly increased to three or four hundred people. Generally, these feasts consisted of:

> *purīs* – a light, tortillalike whole-wheat bread fried
> in ghee
> *pushpanna* rice – an opulent rice dish prepared
> with nuts and spices
> *samosās* – fried pastries stuffed with cauliflower or
> potato and peas

pakorās – vegetables dipped in chickpea batter and
    deep-fried in ghee
two or more *sabjis* – cooked vegetables, often including
    small cubes of fresh, homemade cheese
kheer – a dessert of sweetened condensed milk
burfi – a milk sweet resembling vanilla fudge
lassi – a cooling yogurt-fruit drink

In 1967 Hare Kṛṣṇa devotees opened their second temple, in San Francisco's Haight-Ashbury district, where they served *prasāda* meals free to over 250 people daily. By the early 1970s the ISKCON Sunday feast had been established as a weekly event in major cities throughout the world, including New York, Boston, Washington D.C., San Francisco, Los Angeles, San Diego, Mexico City, Montreal, London, Paris, Rome, Amsterdam, Frankfurt, Nairobi, Calcutta, Bombay, Sydney, Melbourne, and Rio de Janeiro. Sunday feasts continue in almost every ISKCON center the world over. Śrīla Prabhupāda often lightheartedly referred to the Hare Kṛṣṇa movement as "the kitchen religion," thus expressing his satisfaction with how well his followers were carrying out his desire to flood the world with *prasāda*.

Festivals

In addition to serving *prasāda* each Sunday at ISKCON temples, devotees also began to bring their spiritual vegetarian food out to the public in a variety of ways. Ever since the days of Woodstock, devotees have set up *prasāda* kitchens at outdoor gatherings to provide sumptuous free vegetarian food. Devotees have served thousands of plates of *prasāda* at events such as the California US Festival, the Glastonbury Festival near Stonehenge, England, the New Zealand Sweetwaters festival, large-scale national peace rallies in Western Germany, all over Poland, including at the Polish Woodstock Festival through Krishna's Village of Peace, and cultural festivals throughout Central and South America. ISKCON members regularly set up *prasāda* booths at fairs and health- or food-related conventions. The Hare Kṛṣṇa movement also stages its own massive festivals, such as Ratha-yātrā (the Festival of the Chariots), held annually in many major cities around the world. At each event, devotees distribute tens of thousands of plates of delicious vegetarian food. Scott Smith, former associate editor of the *Vegetarian Times*, remarked, "The Hare Kṛṣṇa cooks are the only mass preparers of foodstuffs who maintain such an extraordinarily and consistently high quality of culinary excellence, even when catering to as many as twelve thousand people at a go." When members of ISKCON's Los Angeles center catered a vegetarian luncheon at a celebrity tennis tournament for the National Kidney Foundation, the tournament chairman wrote that the food's "tastiness and healthfulness was all excellent."

Restaurants

By the early 1980s, members of the Hare Kṛṣṇa movement had opened restaurants (usually called Govinda's) in places such as Paris, London, Bombay, Melbourne, Sydney, New York, San Francisco, San Diego, Toronto, Montreal, and Prabhupāda's Palace of Gold, in West Virginia. Each restaurant had built up a steady, satisfied clientele, and restaurant reviewers had given unqualified praise in leading magazines and newspapers.

Now there are several restaurants in the United Kingdom and Ireland, most notably in London, Swansea, and Dublin. The Dublin restaurant, Govinda's, has received a number of rave reviews, including a listing in *The Dubliner 100 Best Restaurants. The Evening Herald* writes, "How about a cheap and cheerful city café-cum-restaurant that's mentioned favourably in almost every Dublin guidebook? ... throw in a remarkably happy kitchen staff, a relaxed eating environment, and a marvelous menu.... Each mouthful was a revelation.... Needless to say, we left Govinda's full-bellied ... and almost as happy as the kitchen staff. Now that's what we call the Om factor!" *The Irish Times* writes, "Good mood food is what you find at Govinda's on Aungier Street, Dublin. The ... Hare Krishnas make their food with serious devotion – it's food to peace out with."

Govinda's in Swansea has been similarly appreciated: "[The food] was different but delicious.... It's relaxing, great value, and the food always feels light, fresh, and cleansing." (*South Wales Evening Post*). The London Govinda's was listed as "a restaurant of tranquillity, health, and balance."

Hare Kṛṣṇa restaurants in the U.S. have received the same positive reviews – Kalachandji's in Dallas (called by one reviewer "a pleasant – no, make that wonderful – surprise"), Govinda's Natural Foods in Los Angeles (referred to by the *Los Angeles Times* as "food of the gods"), Detroit ("A feast of food, a feast of culture, and a feast of happiness").

Nowadays, ISKCON has over ninety restaurants worldwide. Although all ISKCON restaurants strive to offer their clientele a sublime atmosphere for dining, their main business is to provide high quality, healthful, delicious *prasāda* at a cost everyone can afford.

Food for Thought

The members of the Hare Kṛṣṇa movement have introduced *prasāda* to millions of people throughout the world. Along with the sacred food, they have widely distributed the most essential books of Vedic knowledge, such as the *Bhagavad-gītā*, *Śrīmad-Bhāgavatam*, and *Caitanya-caritāmṛta*, which fully explain the law of karma, the doctrine of *ahiṁsā* (nonviolence), and other foundations of a truly spiritual approach to vegetarianism. We urge you to read these books to deepen your understanding of the science of Kṛṣṇa consciousness, of which sacred eating is a major part.

Centers of the International Society for Krishna Consciousness

Founder-Ācārya: His Divine Grace A.C. Bhaktivedanta Swami Prabhupāda

For further information on classes, programs, festivals, residential courses, and local meetings, please contact the center nearest you. This is a partial list. For a full list please contact one of the addresses or visit www.iskcon.com or www.krishna.com

CANADA

Brampton-Mississauga, Ontario — 6 George Street South, 2nd Floor, L6Y 1P3/ Tel. (416) 648-3312/ iskconbrampton@gmail.com

Calgary, Alberta — 313 Fourth St. N.E., T2E 3S3/ Tel. (403) 265-3302/ vamanstones@shaw.ca

Edmonton, Alberta — 9353 35th Ave. NW, T6E 5R5/ Tel. (780) 439-9999/ harekrishna.edmonton@gmail.com

Montreal, Quebec — 1626 Pie IX Blvd., H1V 2C5/ Tel. (514) 521-1301/ iskconmontreal@gmail.com

◆ **Ottawa, Ontario** — 212 Somerset St. E., K1N 6V4/ Tel. (613) 565-6544/ iskconottawa@sympatico.ca

Regina, Saskatchewan — 1279 Retallack St., S4T 2H8/ Tel. (306) 525-0002 or -6461/ jagadishadas@yahoo.com

Scarborough, Ontario — 3500 McNicoll Avenue, Unit #3, M1V4C7/ Tel. (416) 300 7101/ iskconscarborough@hotmail.com

Toronto, Ontario — 243 Avenue Rd., M5R 2J6/ Tel. (416) 922-5415/ toronto@iskcon.net

Vancouver, B.C. — 5462 S.E. Marine Dr., Burnaby V5J 3G8/ Tel. (604) 433-9728/ ISKCONVancouver@gmail.com

RURAL COMMUNITY

Ashcroft, B.C. — Saranagati Dhama (mail: P.O. Box 99, V0K 1A0)/ Tel. (250) 457-7438/ Fax: (250) 453-9306/ iskconsaranagati@hotmail.com

U.S.A.

◆ **Atlanta, Georgia** — 1287 South Ponce de Leon Ave. N.E., 30306/ Tel. (404) 377-8680/ admin@atlantaharekrishnas.com

Austin, Texas — 10700 Jonwood Way, 78753/ Tel. (512) 835-2121/ sda@backtohome.com

Baltimore, Maryland —200 Bloomsbury Ave., Catonsville, 21228/ Tel. (410) 744-1624/ contact@iskconbaltimore.org

Berkeley, California — 2334 Stuart St., 94705/ Tel. (510) 540-9215/ info@iskconberkeley.net

Boise, Idaho — 1615 Martha St., 83706/ Tel. (208) 344-4274/ boise_temple@yahoo.com

Boston, Massachusetts — 72 Commonwealth Ave., 02116/ Tel. (617) 247-8611/ info@iskconboston.org

Chicago, Illinois — 1716 W. Lunt Ave., 60626/ Tel. (773) 973-0900/ chicagoiskcon@yahoo.com

Columbus, Ohio — 379 W. Eighth Ave., 43201/ Tel. (614) 421-1661/ premvilasdas.rns@gmail.com

◆ **Dallas, Texas** — 5430 Gurley Ave., 75223/ Tel. (214) 827-6330/ info@radhakalachandji.com

◆ **Denver, Colorado** — 1400 Cherry St., 80220/ Tel. (303) 333-5461/ info@krishnadenver.com

Detroit, Michigan — 383 Lenox Ave., 48215/ Tel. (313) 824-

6000/ gaurangi108@hotmail.com

Gainesville, Florida — 214 N.W. 14th St., 32603/ Tel. (352) 336-4183/ kalakantha.acbsp@pamho.net

Hartford, Connecticut — 1683 Main St., E. Hartford 06108/ Tel. (860) 289-7252/ pyari108@ gmail.com

Hillsboro, Oregon — 612 North 1st Ave., Hillsboro, 97124/ Tel: (503) 567-7363/ info@iskconportland.com

◆ **Honolulu, Hawaii** — Honolulu, Hawaii — 51 Coelho Way, 96817/ Tel. (808) 595-4913/ hawaii.iskcon@gmail.com

Houston, Texas — 1320 W. 34th St., 77018/ Tel. (713) 686-4482/ management@iskconhouston.org

Kansas City, Missouri — 5201 Paseo Blvd., 64110/ Tel. (816) 924-5619/ rvc@rvc.edu

Laguna Beach, California — 285 Legion St., 92651/ Tel. (949) 494-7029/ info@lagunatemple.com

◆ **Los Angeles, California** — 3764 Watseka Ave., 90034/ Tel. (310) 836-2676/ membership@ harekrishnala.com

Mountain View, California — 1965 Latham St., 94040/ Tel. (650) 336-7993/ isvconnect@gmail.com

◆ **Miami, Florida** — 3220 Virginia St., 33133 (mail: 3109 Grand Ave. #491, Coconut Grove, FL 33133)/ Tel. (305) 461-1348/ devotionalservice@iskcon-miami.com

New Orleans, Louisiana — 2936 Esplanade Ave., 70119/ Tel. (504) 304-0032 (office) or (504) 638-1944 (temple) / gopal211@aol.com

◆ **New York, New York** — 305 Schermerhorn St., Brooklyn 11217/ Tel. (718) 855-6714/ ramabhadra@aol.com

Orlando, Florida — 2651 Rouse Rd., 32817/ Tel. (407) 257-3865/ info@iskconorlando.com

Philadelphia, Pennsylvania — 41 West Allens Lane, 19119/ Tel. (215) 247-4600/ Fax: (215) 247-8702/ savecows@aol.com

◆ **Philadelphia, Pennsylvania** — 1408 South St., 19146/ Tel. (215) 985-9303/ info@iskconphiladelphia.com

Phoenix, Arizona — 100 S. Weber Dr., Chandler, 85226/ Tel. (480) 705-4900/ premadhatridd@gmail.com

Plainfield, New Jersey — 1020 W. 7th St., 07063/ Tel. (973) 519-3374/ harekrsna@iskconnj.com

◆ **St. Louis, Missouri** — 3926 Lindell Blvd., 63108/ Tel. (314) 535-8085 or 534-1708/ rpsdas@gmail.com

Salt Lake City, Utah — 965 E. 3370 South, 84106/ Tel. (801) 487-4005/ utahkrishnas@gmail.com

San Antonio, Texas — 6772 Oxford Trace, 78240/ Tel. (210) 420-1182/ aadasa@gmail.com

◆ **San Diego, California** — 1030 Grand Ave., Pacific Beach 92109/ Tel. (858) 429-9375/ krishna.sandiego@gmail.com

Seattle, Washington — 1420 228th Ave. S.E., Sammamish 98075/ Tel. (425) 246-8436/ info@vediculturalcenter.org

◆ **Spanish Fork, Utah** — Krishna Temple Project & KHQN

Radio, 8628 S. State Rd., 84660/ Tel. (801) 798-3559/ carudas@earthlink.net
Tallahassee, Florida — 4601 Crawfordville Rd., 32305/ Tel. 850-727-5785/ tallahassee.iskcon@gmail.com
Towaco, New Jersey — 100 Jacksonville Rd., 07082/ Tel. (973) 299-0970/ madhupati.jas@pamho.net
◆ **Tucson, Arizona** — 711 E. Blacklidge Dr., 85719/ Tel. (520) 792-0630/ sandaminidd@cs.com
Washington, D.C. — 10310 Oaklyn Dr., Potomac, Maryland 20854/ Tel. (301) 299-2100/ info@iskconofdc.org
RURAL COMMUNITIES
◆ **Alachua, Florida** (New Raman Reti) — 17306 N.W. 112th Blvd., 32615 (mail: P.O. Box 819, 32616)/ Tel. (386) 462-2017/ Fax: (386) 462-2641/ alachuatemple@gmail.com
Carriere, Mississippi (New Talavan) — 31492 Anner Road, 39426/ Tel. (601) 213-3586/ newtalavan@gmail.com
Gurabo, Puerto Rico (New Govardhana Hill) — Carr. 181, Km. 16.3, Bo. Santa Rita, Gurabo (mail: HC-01, Box 8440, Gurabo, PR 00778)/ Tel. (787) 367-3530 or (787) 737-1722/ manonatha@gmail.com
Hillsborough, North Carolina (New Goloka) — 1032 Dimmocks Mill Rd., 27278/ Tel. (919) 732-6492/ bkgoswami@earthlink.net
◆ **Moundsville, West Virginia** (New Vrindaban) — R.D. No. 1, Box 319, Hare Krishna Ridge, 26041/ Tel. (304) 843-1600; Guesthouse, (304) 845-5905/ mail@newvrindaban.com
Mulberry, Tennessee (Murari-sevaka) — 532 Murari Lane, 37359/ Tel. (931) 759-6888/ murari_sevaka@yahoo.com
Port Royal, Pennsylvania (Gita Nagari) — 534 Gita Nagari Rd./ Tel. (717) 527-4101/ dhruva.bts@pamho.net
Sandy Ridge, North Carolina — Prabhupada Village, 1283 Prabhupada Rd., 27046/ Tel. (336) 593-2322/ madanmohanmohini72@gmail.com
ADDITIONAL RESTAURANTS
Hato Rey, Puerto Rico — Tamal Krishna's Veggie Garden, 131 Eleanor Roosevelt, 00918/ Tel. (787) 754-6959/ tkveggiegarden@aol.com

UNITED KINGDOM AND IRELAND

Belfast, Northern Ireland — Sri Sri Radha-Madhava Mandir, Brooklands, 2A Brooklands Grange, Belfast BT17 0HE/ Tel. +44 (28) 9062 0530/ hk.temple108@gmail.com
Birmingham, England — 84 Stanmore Rd., Edgbaston B16 9TB/ Tel. +44 (121) 420 4999/ iskconbirmingham@gmail.com
Cardiff, Wales — Cafe Atma / The Soul Centre, 40 Crwys Road, Cathays, CF24 4NN/ +44 (29) 20 390 391/ cafe.atma@gmail.com
Coventry, England — Kingfield Rd., Coventry (mail: 19 Gloucester St., Coventry CV1 3BZ)/ Tel. +44 (24) 7655 2822 or -5420/ haridas.kds@pamho.net
◆ **Dublin, Ireland** — 83 Middle Abbey St., Dublin 1/ Tel. +353 (1) 661 5095/ dublin@krishna.ie; Govinda's: info@govindas.ie
Lesmahagow, Scotland — Karuna Bhavan, Bankhouse Rd., Lesmahagow, Lanarkshire, ML11 0ES/ Tel. +44 (1555) 894790/ karunabhavan@aol.com
Leicester, England — 31 Granby Street, LE1 6EP/ Tel. +44 (0) 7597 786 676/ pradyumna.jas@pamho.net
◆ **London, England** (city) — Radha-Krishna Temple, 10 Soho Street, London W1D 3DL/ Tel. +44 (20) 7437 3662; shop, 7440 5221; Govinda's Restaurant, 7440 5229/ info@iskcon-london.com
◆ **London, England** (country) — Bhaktivedanta Manor, Dharam Marg, Hilfield Lane, Watford, Herts, WD25 8EZ/ Tel. +44 (1923) 851000/ info@krishnatemple.com; Guesthouse: bmguesthouse@

krishna.com
London, England (south) — 42 Enmore Road, South Norwood, SE25 5NG/ Tel. +44 7988857530/ krishnaprema89@hotmail.com
London, England (Kings Cross) —102 Caledonain Rd., Kings Cross, Islington, N1 9DN/ Tel. +44 (20) 7168 5732/ foodforalluk@aol.com
Manchester, England — 20 Mayfield Rd., Whalley Range, M16 8FT/ Tel. +44 (161) 226 4416/ contact@iskconmanchester.com
Newcastle-upon-Tyne, England — 304 Westgate Rd., NE4 6AR/ Tel. +44 (191) 272 1911
◆ **Swansea, Wales** — Govinda's, 8 Craddock St., SA1 3EN/ Tel. +44 (1792) 468469/ info@iskconwales.org.uk; restaurant, info@govindas.org.uk
RURAL COMMUNITIES
Upper Lough Erne, Northern Ireland — Govindadwipa Dhama, Inisrath Island, Derrylin, Co. Fermanagh, BT92 9GN/ Tel. +44 (28) 6772 3878/ govindadwipa@pamho.net
London, England — (contact Bhaktivedanta Manor) Programs are held regularly in more than forty other cities in the UK. For information, contact ISKCON Reader Services, P.O. Box 730, Watford WD25 8EZ, UK
ADDITIONAL RESTAURANTS
Dublin, Ireland — Govinda's, 4 Aungier St., Dublin 2/ Tel. +353 (1) 475 0309/ info@govindas.ie
Dublin, Ireland — Govinda's, 18 Merrion Row, Dublin 2/ Tel. +353 (1) 661 5095/ praghosa.sdg@pamho.net
Dublin, Ireland — Govinda's, 83 Middle Abbey St., Dublin 1/ Tel +353 (1) 661 5096/ info@govindas.ie
Nottingham, England — Govinda's Nottingham, 7–9 Thurland Street, NG1 3DR/ Tel. +44 115 985 9639/ govindasnottingham@gmail.com

AUSTRALASIA
AUSTRALIA
Adelaide — 25 Le Hunte St. (mail: P.O. Box 114, Kilburn, SA 5084)/ Tel. +61 (8) 8359-5120/ iskconsa@tpg.com.au
Brisbane — 95 Bank Rd., Graceville (mail: P.O. Box 83, Indooroopilly), QLD 4068/ Tel. +61 (7) 3379-5455/
Canberra — 44 Limestone Ave., Ainslie, ACT 2602 (mail: P.O. Box 1411, Canberra, ACT 2601)/ Tel. +61 (2) 6262-6208/
Melbourne — 197 Danks St. (mail: P.O. Box 125), Albert Park, VIC 3206/ Tel. +61 (3) 9699-5122/ melbourne@pamho.net
Perth — 155-159 Canning Rd., Kalamunda (mail: P.O. Box 201 Kalamunda 6076)/ Tel. +61 (8) 6293-1519/ perth@pamho.net
Sydney — 180 Falcon St., North Sydney, NSW 2060 (mail: P.O. Box 459, Cammeray, NSW 2062)/ Tel. +61 (2) 9959-4558/ admin@iskcon.com.au
Sydney — Govinda's Yoga & Meditation Centre, 112 Darlinghurst Rd., Darlinghurst NSW 2010 (mail: P.O. Box 174, Kings Cross 1340)/ Tel. +61 (2) 9380-5162/ sita@govindas.com.au
RURAL COMMUNITIES
Bambra, VIC (New Nandagram) — 50 Seaches Outlet, off 1265 Winchelsea Deans Marsh Rd., Bambra VIC 3241/ Tel. +61 (3) 5288-7383
Cessnock, NSW (New Gokula) — Lewis Lane, off Mount View Road, Millfield, near Cessnock (mail: P.O. Box 399, Cessnock, NSW 2325)/ Tel. +61 (2) 4998-1800/ Fax: iskconfarm@mac.com
Murwillumbah, NSW (New Govardhana) — Tyalgum Rd., Eungella (mail: P.O. Box 687), NSW 2484/ Tel. +61 (2) 6672-6579/ Fax: +61 (2) 6672-5498/ ajita@in.com.au

RESTAURANTS

Brisbane — Govinda's, 99 Elizabeth St., 1st Floor, QLD 4000/ Tel. +61 (7) 3210-0255

Brisbane — Krishna's Cafe, 1st Floor, 82 Vulture St., West End, QLD 4000/ Tel. +61 (7) 3844-2316/ brisbane@pamho.net

Burleigh Heads — Govinda's, 20 James St., Burleigh Heads, QLD 4220/ Tel. +61 (7) 5607-0782/ ajita@in.com.au

Maroochydore — Govinda's Vegetarian Cafe, 2/7 First Ave., QLD 4558/ Tel. +61 (7) 5451-0299

Melbourne — Crossways, 1st Floor, 123 Swanston St., VIC 3000/ Tel. +61 (3) 9650-2939

Melbourne — Gopal's, 139 Swanston St., VIC 3000/ Tel. +61 (3) 9650-1578

Perth — Govinda's Restaurant, 194 William St., Northbridge, W.A. 6003/ Tel. +61 (8) 9227-1684/ perth@pamho.net

NEW ZEALAND AND FIJI

Auckland, NZ — The Loft, 1st Floor, 103 Beach Rd./ Tel. +64 (9) 3797301

Christchurch, NZ — 83 Bealey Ave. (mail: P.O. Box 25-190)/ Tel. +64 (3) 366-5174/ iskconchch@clear.net.nz

Hamilton, NZ — 188 Maui St., RD 8, Te Rapa/ Tel. +64 (7) 850-5108/ rmaster@wave.co.nz

Labasa, Fiji — Delailabasa (mail: P.O. Box 133)/ Tel. +679 812912

Lautoka, Fiji — 5 Tavewa Ave. (mail: P.O. Box 125)/ Tel. +679 666 4112/ regprakash@excite.com

Nausori, Fiji — Hare Krishna Cultural Centre, 2nd Floor, Shop & Save Building, 11 Gulam Nadi St., Nausori Town (mail: P.O. Box 2183, Govt. Bldgs., Suva)/ Tel. +679 996 9748 or 347 5097/ vdas@frca.org.fj

Rakiraki, Fiji — Rewasa (mail: P.O. Box 204)/ Tel. +679 694243

Sigatoka, Fiji — Queens Rd., Olosara (mail: P.O. Box 1020)/ Tel. +679 9373703 or 6520866/ drgsmarna@connect.com.fj

Suva, Fiji — 166 Brewster St. (mail: P.O. Box 4229, Samabula)/ Tel. +679 331 8441/ iskconsuva@connect.com.fj

Wellington, NZ — 105 Newlands Rd., Newlands/ Tel. +64 (4) 478-4108/ iskconwellington.org.nz

Wellington, NZ — Gaura Yoga Centre, 1st Floor, 175 Vivian St. (mail: P.O. Box 6271, Marion Square)/ Tel. +64 (4) 801-5500/ yoga@gaurayoga.co.nz

RURAL COMMUNITY

Auckland, NZ (New Varshan) — Hwy. 28, Riverhead, next to Huapai Golf Course (mail: R.D. 2, Kumeu)/ Tel. +64 (9) 412-8075

RESTAURANTS

Auckland, NZ — Hare Krishna Food for Life, 268 Karangahape Rd./ Tel. +64 (9) 300-7585

Labasa, Fiji — Hare Krishna Restaurant, Naseakula Road/ Tel. +679 811364

Lautoka, Fiji — Gopal's, Corner of Yasawa Street and Naviti Street/ Tel. +679 662990

Suva, Fiji — Hare Krishna Vegetarian Restaurant, Dolphins FNPF Place, Victoria Parade/ Tel. +679 314154/ vdas@govnet.gov.fj

Suva, Fiji — Hare Krishna Vegetarian Restaurant, Opposite University of the South Pacific, Laucala Bay Rd./ Tel. +679 311683/ vdas@govnet.gov.fj

Suva, Fiji — Hare Krishna Vegetarian Restaurant, 18 Pratt St./ Tel. +679 314154

Suva, Fiji — Hare Krishna Vegetarian Restaurant, 82 Ratu Mara Rd., Samabula/ Tel. +679 386333

Suva, Fiji — Hare Krishna Vegetarian Restaurant, Terry Walk, Cumming St./ Tel. +679 312295

Wellington, NZ — Higher Taste Hare Krishna Restaurant, Old Bank Arcade, Ground Flr., Corner Customhouse, Quay & Hunter St., Wellington/ Tel. +64 (4) 472-2233/ Fax: (4) 472-2234/ highertaste@iskconwellington.org.nz

EUROPE (partial list)

Amsterdam, The Netherlands — Van Hilligaertstraat 17, 1072 JX/ Tel. +31 (20) 675-1404 or -1694/ amsterdam@pamho.net

Bergamo — Villaggio Hare Krishna (da Medolago strada per Terno d'Isola), 24040 Chignolo d'Isola (BG)/ Tel. +39 (035) 4940705/ villagio.hare.krsna@hare.krsna.it

Budapest — Govinda Restaurant, Vigyazo Ferenc St. 4, 1051 Budapest/ Tel. +36 (1) 269-1625 or 302-2284

Copenhagen, Denmark — Skjulhoj Alle 44, 2720 Vanlose, Copenhagen/ Tel. +45 4828 6446/ iskcon.denmark@pamho.net

Grödinge — Radha-Krishna Temple, Korsnäs Gård, 14792 Grödinge/ Tel. +46 (8) 53029800/ bmd@pamho.net

Helsinki, Finland — Ruoholahdenkatu 24 D (III krs) 00180/ Tel. +358 (9) 694-9879 or -9837/ harekrishna@harekrishna.fi

♦ **Lisbon, Portugal** — Rua Dona Estefania, 91 R/C 1000 Lisboa/ Tel. & fax: +351 (1) 314-0314 or 352-0038

Madrid — Espíritu Santo 19, 28004/ Tel. +34 91 521-3096

Paris, France — 230 Avenue de la Division Leclerc, 95200 Sarcelles Village/ Tel. +33 (1) 39885358/ paris@pamho.net

♦ **Radhadesh, Belgium** — Chateau de Petite Somme, 6940 Septon-Durbuy/ Tel. +32 (086) 322926 (restaurant: 321421)/ Fax: +32 (086) 322929/ radhadesh@pamho.net

♦ **Rome** — Govinda Centro Hare Krsna, via Santa Maria del Pianto, 16, 00186/ Tel. +39 (06) 68891540/ govinda.roma@harekrsna.it

♦ **Stockholm** — Fridhemsgatan 22, 11240/ Tel. +46 (8) 654-9002/ Restaurant: Tel. & fax: +46 (8) 654-9004/ lokanatha@hotmail.com

Zürich, Switzerland — Bergstrasse 54, 8032/ Tel. +41 (044) 262 33 88/ kgs@pamho.net

RURAL COMMUNITIES

France (La Nouvelle Mayapura) — Domaine d'Oublaisse, 36360, Lucay le Mâle/ Tel. +33 (2) 5440-2395/ oublaise@free.fr

Germany (Simhachalam) — Passau, Zielberg 20, 94118 Jandelsbrunn/ Tel +49 (8583) 316/ info@simhachalam.de

Hungary (New Vraja-dhama) — Krsna-völgy, Fö u. 38, 8699 Somogyvamos/ Tel. & fax: +36 (85) 540-002 or 340-185/ info@krisnavolgy.hu

Italy (Villa Vrindavan) — Florence, via Scopeti 108, 50026 San Casciano in Val di Pesa (FI)/ Tel. +39 (055) 820054/ isvaripriya@libero.it

Spain (New Vraja Mandala) — (Santa Clara) 19411 Brihuega / Tel. +34 949 280436

ADDITIONAL RESTAURANTS

Barcelona — Restaurante Govinda, Plaza de la Villa de Madrid 4-5, 08002/ Tel. +34 93 318-7729

Copenhagen, Denmark — Govinda's, Nørre Farimagsgade 82, DK-1364 Kbh K/ Tel. +45 3333 7444

Milan — Govinda's, via Valpetrosa 5, 20123/ Tel. +39 (02) 862417

Oslo, Norway — Krishna's Cuisine, Kirkeveien 59B, 0364/ Tel. +47 (22) 606-250

The Authors

Bhūtātmā Dāsa (Austin Gordon, PhD) is a professor of political philosophy and mass communications at California State University, Fullerton. After taking initiation from His Divine Grace A. C. Bhaktivedanta Swami Prabhupāda in 1971, he traveled extensively throughout India and the Far East for seven years studying spiritual traditions and meditation. He later served in ISKCON's Office of Public Affairs. Along with publishing articles in his academic discipline, Bhūtātmā has co-authored and authored several books on Eastern thought, including *Coming Back: The Science of Reincarnation*, *Chant and Be Happy*, and *The Eye of the Storm: The Power of the Undisturbed Mind*.

Kūrma Dāsa is one of the world's leading proponents of pure vegetarian cuisine. Dubbed – Australia's Vegetarian Guru," Kūrma has been writing cookbooks, teaching students, and hosting internationally broadcast TV shows for over thirtyfive years. Kūrma's innovative cooking continues to shake off the outdated notion that vegetarian food is lackluster. He lives in Perth, Australia. The lucidly explained recipes in each of Kūrma's four cookbooks provide an adventure in world culture, taste, and nutrition. He has also published two recipe-card sets, – Quick Vegetarian Cards" and – Cooking With Kurma Vegi Cards."
For more information, visit www.kurma.net

Drutakarmā Dāsa (Michael A. Cremo) is a researcher in the history of science for the Bhaktivedanta Institute, the science studies branch of the International Society for Krishna Consciousness (ISKCON). He has presented papers on Vedic environmental philosophy at international conferences and is also the author of *Human Devolution: A Vedic Alternative to Darwin's Theory* and *Forbidden Archaeology* (with Richard L. Thompson). He has lectured at the Royal Institution in London, the Russian Academy of Science in Moscow, and other scientific institutions and universities throughout the world. He is a member of the History of Science Society, the Philosophy of Science Association, and the World Archaeological Congress. Born in 1948, he became an initiated disciple of His Divine Grace A. C. Bhaktivedanta Swami Prabhupāda in 1976.

Mukunda Goswami, writer, researcher, editor, and one of the earliest members of the International Society for Krishna Consciousness, has lectured in thirtyeight countries and published newspaper and magazine articles on spirituality and contemporary issues. Co-author of four books, including *Divine Nature: A Spiritual Perspective on the Environmental Crisis* and *Coming Back: The Science of Reincarnation,* he now resides in New Zealand, where he continues to write.